Virtual Reality, Augmented Reality and Artificial Intelligence in Special Education

New technologies and ongoing developments in the fields of Virtual Reality, Augmented Reality and Artificial Intelligence are changing the ways in which we facilitate learning. Recognising the positive role these technologies can play in the learning and progress of students assessed as having special educational needs, this practical guide explains the characteristics, benefits, risks and potential applications of new technologies in the classroom.

An innovative and timely resource, *Virtual Reality, Augmented Reality and Artificial Intelligence in Special Education* offers a background in the evidence-based theory and practice of using new technologies in an educational context. Accessible and free of complex jargon, chapters provide information on the development, intended uses and most current terminology used in relation to technologies, and explains how modern equipment, approaches and possibilities can be used to promote improved communication skills, independent learning and heightened self-esteem amongst students diagnosed with SEND. Offering a wealth of practical tips, downloadable resources and ideas for engaging with technology in the classroom, the text will support teachers to ensure that students can benefit from exciting technological advances and learn to use them appropriately.

Demystifying a complex and varied field, this practical resource will inspire and inform teachers, SENCOs and practitioners working with children and students with SEND as they harness the use of technology in the classroom.

Ange Anderson is Headteacher of a Special school for pupils aged 2–11.

Virtual Reality, Augmented Reality and Artificial Intelligence in Special Education

A Practical Guide to Supporting Students with Learning Differences

Ange Anderson

Routledge
Taylor & Francis Group

LONDON AND NEW YORK

First published 2019
by Routledge
2 Park Square, Milton Park, Abingdon, Oxon OX14 4RN

and by Routledge
52 Vanderbilt Avenue, New York, NY 10017

Routledge is an imprint of the Taylor & Francis Group, an informa business

British Library Cataloguing-in-Publication Data
A catalogue record for this book is available from the British Library

Library of Congress Cataloging-in-Publication Data
A catalog record has been requested for this book

ISBN: 9780367145323 (hbk)
ISBN: 9780367024536 (pbk)
ISBN: 9780429399503 (ebk)

Typeset in Optima
by Servis Filmsetting Ltd, Stockport, Cheshire
Printed and bound by CPI Group (UK) Ltd, Croydon, CR0 4YY

Visit: www.routledge.com/9780367024536

Dedication

This book is dedicated to all children who struggle in school with an inappropriate education.

Contents

Acknowledgments

Some passages in the present work are adapted from my works published on LinkedIn. Another passage is adapted from my article for the *Journal of Research in Special Educational Needs* Volume 16.

I am very grateful to all of the staff at Ysgol Pen Coch, a special school in Flint, North Wales. I am constantly researching new therapies that may enable our students to be in the right frame of mind to learn, as well as the latest technologies that support their communication. When I am confident that these could benefit our students, that we can raise the funds needed and staff volunteer to be trained in their delivery, we introduce them into the school. The success that we have seen is due in part to the passion of the staff of Ysgol Pen Coch. Thank you.

List of figures

List of tables and downloadable resources

Introduction

I have a dream was a speech delivered by Martin Luther King in 1963. In that speech he said "I have a dream that my four little children will one day live in a nation where they will not be judged by the colour of their skin but by the content of their character". His vision came to fruition.

Many students with autism, attention deficient hyperactive disorder and other neurological conditions, who can speak for themselves, do not see themselves as having learning disabilities because these conditions are not solely related to learning. Also these conditions can have strengths as well as weaknesses.

How do you view disability and how do you think students classed as having learning disabilities wish to be viewed?

Edward Khanya Ndopo was described by the press in 2009 as "A remarkable young black man who is severely disabled and confined to a wheelchair". Edward Khanya Ndopo does not have communication issues and was able to reply.

He wrote:

> In this regard, let me make an emphatic point of correction. (1) I am not disabled; I live with a disability. The former defines me by my limitations whereas the latter defines me in spite of my limitations. (2) I am not confined to a wheelchair; I use a wheelchair for mobility. The former suggests that I have been imprisoned to a life of misery on "wheels" whereas the latter confirms that my "wheels" have in actual fact given me a life of relative independence. And (3), it is crucial to make these corrections, for they go beyond the semantics of political correctness. These corrections are made in order to tell a different story from the one we're used to — a story of a world in which the content of one's character supersedes that of one's physical appearance.
>
> (Ndopo, Edward K (2009))

I recall a few years ago having to park my car some distance away from my father's home. As I walked along the pavement towards his home, I saw an elderly man walking towards me from quite a distance away and I was struck by how difficult he was finding the walk, even with the aid of a stick. As I got nearer to my father's home I realised that the elderly man was my father. I was suddenly overcome with the realisation that my father was old yet 'the content of his character had superseded his physical appearance'.

Working in a special school is a privilege where you are lucky to meet some amazing, resilient students and the content of their characters would enthral you. The technologies that we have introduced into the school have changed the way that we facilitate learning. Students who would not previously be able to communicate now can. There is a technological revolution going on and even today, as I write, something new in technology could change the lives of our students forever. Then society can no longer look at them as learning disabled because we are able to say that their learning has been enabled by technology.

Exciting times.

The fourth Industrial Revolution

This is the most exciting time in history to be alive. We are going through the fourth Industrial Revolution (Schwab 2017). Industrial Revolutions are exciting times of change that have huge impact on the human race. They transform how people live, work and communicate.

If we look to history and the time it took the human race to have its first Industrial Revolution, we would be amazed. It didn't happen until 1765! Archaeological discoveries tell us that wheels were created to serve as potter's wheels around 3500 B.C. (Gambino 2009) – 5265 years before someone figured out how to use them as a mechanical spinning wheel.

The first Industrial Revolution began with the emergence of mechanisation. The second Industrial Revolution began approximately a hundred years later in 1870 with the emergence of new sources of energy – electricity, gas and oil – and was the age of science and mass production. The third Industrial Revolution began a hundred years after that in 1969 with the emergence of nuclear energy – and the digital age began. We are now going through the fourth Industrial Revolution and it's only 50 years on.

Today technological advancements are happening on a daily basis and they are unstoppable. I believe the big five well-known giants leading this transformation are Google, Microsoft, Apple, Facebook and Amazon. They are ploughing billions of dollars into the technological revolution. I recently returned from the technology festival TechXLR8 in London and I can confirm that there are many other lesser known companies biting at their heels to get some of the action.

This unstoppable change has been the case with every industrial revolution, beginning with the invention of the mechanical spinning wheel and the steam engine. I have found in my job, as a head teacher of a special school, that it is not only the students with autism who find change difficult. Ordinary humans do too. The advantage that we have today with the fourth Industrial Revolution is that we know far more than we did then and should be able to plan for change with better insight.

Education in Britain has been stuck in the rut of aiming for university for every child yet students' strengths have always been very different. Universally, governments are realising that traditional instructional learning is not working with regard to future employment requirements.

Students who are neurodiverse can offer abilities and strengths to the future work-force. Many of the students in our school show strong abilities with computers and technology. Some of our students show above-average attention to detail and can think "outside of the box".

If we looked back in the history books we would find that some people who were neu-rodiverse managed to help change history in spite of their education – Thomas Edison, for instance. Edison was schooled at home, having failed at an ordinary school. Today the classroom is no longer restricted to a location or certain hours in a day but is an experience that can happen virtually anywhere, at any time of the day or night. Online learning is already with us. The virtual classroom is already with us. Thomas Edison was a child of his time but I believe someone like him would thrive in this digital age.

The fourth Revolution will bring ethical dilemmas with its advances. Leaders in myoelectric prosthesis are providing highly functional bionic hands and arms for disa-bled people. The thinking is that if you are going to have a prosthesis then make it even better than an ordinary limb. 3D printing is widely applied in prosthesis development now, which significantly reduces the cost. They also use a rehabilitation system for using prostheses that applies VR.

Can you imagine a student with a prosthetic arm in class who cannot only do the same as any other ordinary student but will also have the advantage of wi-fi access, built-in-touch-screen, voice search and will be able to respond to messages, play music, shop, link to game consoles and a host of other possible advantages? No longer will that student be looked upon with sympathy or criticism for being different but that student may well become the most popular student in the class. But with advantage comes responsibility. Do we as teachers need to teach the student with the prosthetic arm to use those advantages responsibly? Do we as teachers need to teach all students to use the advantages of a mobile phone responsibly. Should we be prepared to teach all stu-dents in the future to use their smartglasses responsibly?

In the future the virtual world and the real world will be so entwined that people already call it mixed reality. Instead of using our hands to turn on a phone we will just need to move our eyes to make things happen. In fact, people are already hav-ing implants put in their eyes so that their brainwaves can take charge (Dube 2014). Already holograms are available to those who can afford the technology. In the near future instead of Skyping with family members it will be possible for their hologram to appear in the same room and we may even be able to touch them through haptic technology.

As this new technology takes over the world, it allows for flexibility in some work-forces. In our school we have a good number of staff who work part-time to ensure they have the work/life balance that they want. Flexibility in the workplace is key to the wellbeing of staff. Today, technology allows some workers to work from home some of the time. How can we recreate this kind of flexibility in schools where for hundreds of years the school day has remained the same?

Should school opening times change? Should we give school staff the same kind of flexibility that other workforces take for granted? Or should we find ways that technology can support us in schools to make the job less stressful and more enjoyable? Virtual reality, augmented reality and artificial intelligence may well hold the keys. These technologies will support teachers in their role by the development of automating technologies that enable humans to be more effective and efficient.

Governments across the world are changing education policy and spending millions on reform and professional development. It is up to teachers to take up the training offered by the local authorities, governments and also by the tech giants already mentioned to ensure they know how to take advantage of this new technology.

These technologies combined with the many talents of teachers today provide opportunities to revolutionise education.

2 | What is VR, AR and AI?

Virtual reality

Virtual reality (VR) can mean different things to different people. I was recently chatting with a mother and her son (who uses a wheelchair for mobility and attends a mainstream school). They were at our special school so that he could access the hydrotherapy pool. "John managed to raise a hundred pounds by walking up Snowdon yesterday," she told me.

I looked to John for confirmation. The 13-year-old told me, "I worked out the distance the other students would be walking and divided that by the perimeter of

Figure 2.1 School football pitch 2018

the school's football pitch and then I wheeled myself around the pitch until I completed an equivalent challenge." I call it the "virtual walk". It takes tenacity to ensure that you are in some way involved in the same challenging experience as your fellow classmates and John was able to say he had taken part and raised money in the process.

Virtual reality from the technological perspective is the means for creating the illusion that you are in a different place. It is like being really present in a dream. Virtual reality can immerse us in totally new, synthetic worlds with 360° views. It replaces the real world with a simulated one that incorporates sensory feedback, mainly auditory, visual and haptic.

It is the means for helping people go to that unfamiliar place while on a treadmill, in an armchair, in a wheelchair, in the home or school or office without physically having to travel there because now there are apps available that are set up to follow along a virtual path via Google Maps or similar means.

Some apps work with your tablet or smartphone on these interactive scenic tours. There are also videos and DVDs you can use for your TV, tablet or via an app to give you a virtual walking experience.

The videos can take you on virtual scenic walks in gorgeous places around the world. These virtual experiences can detect your speed, so that your "walk" slows down and speeds up as you do. You can also learn facts about the different locales. If John's school had had VR headsets, John could have had possibly an even better virtual experience.

Figure 2.2 Snowdon miner's path 2018

VR can also take you to the dinosaur Age, to the Moon, or a DC comic Universe, with or without superpowers. It is the means for taking you to a fantastical make-believe world waiting to be explored and for you to play a role, creating an experience that is not possible in ordinary physical reality. Robert Louis Stevenson, who wrote *The Land of Counterpane*[1] in 1885 referring to his childhood imaginings whilst bedridden, may well have enjoyed the opportunity to enter the VR world.

The term "virtual reality" was coined by Jaron Lanier in 1987 during a period of intense research activity into this form of technology. Even though NASAs research into VR interested other researchers, virtual reality was not introduced to the general public until 1989. Jaron Lanier, the founder of VPL Research Company, defined it as "a computer generated, interactive, three-dimensional environment in which a person is immersed". In his book *Dawn of the New Everything* (2017) he goes on to give 47 different definitions. Ironically VPL named it the eye- phone. In those days the eye-phone system, including the computers required to run it, cost upwards of $250,000.

Regardless of its cost, virtual reality captured the public imagination and lots of work has been done since 1989 to explore the possibilities of virtual reality in new areas of application such as military, medicine and the motor industry. Although virtual reality technology has been developing over this seemingly long period, the possibilities for education through this new medium have only recently taken off, partly due to the wait for Moore's Law[2] to allow computation to get cheaper and more available.

Computer scientist Ivan Sutherland developed the first VR headset in 1968. In 2016, nearly 89 million VR headsets were sold worldwide and 98% were of the mobile VR headset type.

The most talked about VR system on the market today is probably Oculus Rift. It was first launched as a Kickstarter project in 2012 and was acquired by Facebook in 2014.

Samsung partnered with Oculus in September 2014 to build a Samsung Gear VR which is powered by Samsung mobile phones. Samsung Gear VR sold around 2.317 million devices in 2017.

Sony have combined their VR headset with their famous gaming hardware PlayStation and named it Sony PlayStation VR.

HTC Vive launched in 2016 with the much-acclaimed Tilt Brush as one of its applications. Tilt Brush is a room-scale VR 3D painting application that presents the user with a virtual palette. Using a hand-held controller the user can create brush strokes of colour in the virtual environment.

Apple has a good selection of iPhone VR apps in its App store and these can be used on any iPhone that is running iOS 11.[3] You also need to purchase a VR headset.

Google Cardboard headsets currently have the major share of the market and in 2016 had 84 million devices. Google Cardboard was initiated as an experiment to let people experience virtual reality. Google was able to corner the market due to its cheap price and early release. A mobile phone is also needed.

ClassVR was launched at the Bett Show in London in January 2017 by Avantis.

ClassVR is now available in the UK, Middle East, Australia, China and the United States. ClassVR's headset is a standalone, classroom-ready device, delivering a fully immersive VR experience under the teacher's control.

Google, in partnership with others, have also brought out standalone headsets that understands your movement in space without the need to set-up any external sensors. Our school has purchased a set of these from RedBox.[4]

VR is probably most used in the games industry. The VR gaming market is now big business. There are gaming centres and eSport arenas opening up all over America. The events that they host can accompany or replace traditional sports. Parents accompany younger players and are amazed at the abilities their children have in the "sport". The International eSports Federation (IeSF) claim that the Paris 2024 Olympic organisers are now in talks about including gaming as a demonstration sport at the Olympic Games (BBC 2018). The International Olympic Committee (IOC) president said gaming "could be considered a sporting activity" but "must not infringe" on Olympic values in order to be recognised as a sport. In 2020 it is estimated that the VR software revenue would reach 20 billion dollars.

In this day and age, when our homes are powered by broadband, technology is ever-present, and gaming is being considered as an Olympic sport because of its popularity, schools can use this obsession to reach and educate students.[5]

VR in schools allows students to visualise abstract concepts and to visit environments and interact with events that distance, time or safety factors make unavailable.

For instance, virtual language labs allow students to have a conversation with a native speaker without leaving the room, while virtual science labs allow students to experiment without open flames or dangerous chemicals. Google and Labster have developed many immersive lab experiences for the Daydream platform that universities and colleges have adopted. Students can access these online virtual labs at any time and as many times as they need to.

Google Arts and Culture,[6] dedicated to help preserve and make accessible art from around the world uses interactive media like VR tours to allow students in schools (and the general public) access to great works of art from the classroom. At least 1,500 museums from over 70 countries have partnered with Google Arts and Culture to put their collections online.

One only has to go to a search engine online to see a surge in companies solely dedicated to provide packaged curriculum and content, teacher training and technological tools to support VR-based instruction in schools.

Sometimes those involved in creating virtual reality experiences are also preserving heritage and history. In 2016 there was an earthquake in the province of Myanmar. The temple Ananda Ok Kyaung in Bagan suffered damage. Fortunately, CyArk had managed to laser map the site prior to the disaster, and now students can take an interactive 3D tour through the temple as it was prior to its destruction. CyARK has partnered with Google Arts and Culture to give students these experiences.

Figure 2.3 AR convention London 2018

Second Life is a free online virtual world that, according to Daniel Voyager's blog (2018) has over 55 million users. In the virtual world of Second Life® (SL), people with disabilities have a chance to experience life beyond the limitations of their disabilities. In virtual worlds, computer-simulated environments host avatars, which are digital representations of a specific person. The avatar can manipulate objects and participate in day-to-day activities that most people take for granted, such as walking, dancing, and communicating. VR can help increase feelings of self-worth and empowerment for those with disabilities.

Psychologists and other medical professionals are using VR to heighten traditional therapy methods and find effective solutions for treatments of PTSD, anxiety and social disorders. Doctors are employing VR to train medical students in surgery, treat patients' pains and even help paraplegics regain body functions.

Augmented reality (AR)

The term "augmented reality" was coined by Boeing researcher Thomas Caudell in 1990. He used the term in relation to the industrial use of AR at Boeing. Since 1990 different industries have been involved in research and the development of AR.

Augmented Reality became a more familiar term for the general public during the Pokémon GO craze in 2016 when a re-imagined a mid-1990s computer game was launched as an AR app that allowed users to catch digital creatures in real locations. Pokémon GO combines locational data with a digital world in a way that creates a wholly new and meaningful experience that could not have existed otherwise. Like pretty much every AR game, Pokémon Go uses your phone's camera to place an image of a Pokémon within your surroundings, and the GPS, accelerometer and compass give the game an idea of which direction your phone is pointing toward.

It took the radio 38 years to reach a market audience of 50 million. It took Pokeman Go 19 days (Scott 2018).

New Zealander Tom Currie, a full-time Pokémon trainer recalls: "I met a woman at the very bottom of New Zealand. … Her son had autism, and she said he was out walking more in the first day of Pokémon Go than he had in an entire year" (Robinson 2016).

AR may be considered a form of VR but where wearers of smartglasses continue to be in touch with the real world while interacting with virtual objects around them. What makes AR very different from VR is that it is designed to be part of the wearer's reality instead of taking the wearer into a different reality.

HP reveal and QR codes

When you watch a sport on TV nowadays you often see the sporting arena marked out using 4K/UHD real-time graphics solutions, to produce overlays onto the pitch. It has been "augmented" with additional computer-generated elements. You can create augmented reality experiences with a free app for iOS or android if you go to an app store. You can also make your own overlays to create a PowerPoint presentation using their website at: www.hpreveal.com/ You can link the augmented reality experience to a QR code so that when a student uses a phone or iPad and hovers over the QR code a 3D experience happens.

QR stands for quick response. These codes have been very popular for introducing AR into the classroom in recent years. It's very similar to a bar code. They originated

Figure 2.4 QR code

in Japan at the Toyota factory. We are all used to seeing bar codes on products in the supermarket. If it's self- service, then you will have scanned the bar code for yourself and the cost of the product will appear on the screen in front of you.

A QR code is more versatile than that. It allows you to store any kind of information that you like. You can get a free scanner reader app from an app store that you save onto your phone. It will pick up QR codes and will bring up some kind of media such as a website, video or audio recording. You just need to hold the phone up to the code to scan it and it takes you there. You can make your own QR codes for free by going to websites such as: www.qr-code-generator.com/

When on the website you can choose a free option from URLs for websites; V card for saving contacts to your smartphone; plain text to allow you to write what you like; email and SMS messages. I made the QR code at the top of this paragraph and if you scan it, it will take you to our school website.

Smartglasses

AugmentedReality.org claims that AR smartglasses will displace the smartphone market, with 1 billion shipments sometime between 2019 and 2023. An example of smartglasses can be seen in Figure 2.5. AR smartglasses have the potential to impact on our world in a similar way to smartphones. The key benefit of smartglasses is that there will no longer be a need for display devices, creating freedom for your hands to interact with the world. TVs and computer monitors could all be replaced by smart-glasses. The look of the glasses has long been a concern to developers. People like wearing sunglasses but often dislike wearing ordinary glasses. Many of the new smart-glasses look like designer sunglasses, making them an attractive addition to someone's wardrobe.

Microsoft HoloLens was released in 2016 and was the world's first self-contained AR holographic computer. HoloLens are AR smartglasses. They have built-in sensors that let you use your gaze to move the cursor so you can select holograms. If you turn your head, the cursor will follow. You can interact with HoloLens by using simple gestures to open apps, documents, spreadsheets, photo albums etc. and select and size items to see them in front of you or push them further away. You can also access the web.

Figure 2.5 Smartglasses

Using HoloLens, you can drag and drop holograms anywhere in your world. Using the holographic frame, centred in the middle of view, preserves your peripheral vision so that you can connect and collaborate with the world around you. Holograms and AR don't block out what you can see and hear. This enables you to work with digital content and tools alongside things in the real world. Holograms can be locked in place or they can travel with you.

You can have as many monitors and as many TVs in front of you using HoloLens. You can use voice commands to navigate, select, open, command and control your apps. You can speak directly to Cortana, who can help you to complete tasks. It remains very expensive at this present time but is also available to have on lease.

Greg Sullivan, Microsoft's Director of Communications said in an interview in 2018 that "In its current model, HoloLens is a commercial product for businesses and the enterprise, not for consumers" (Wong 2018). Other companies have brought out similar smartglasses that are being used in industry. Some popular versions are: ODG's R-9 smartglasses, Sony smart eye glass, Vuzix M3000, Atheer AIR, Magic Leap 1 and Cast AR.

Google unveiled AR smartglasses in 2012 but they were very expensive at $1500, and Google discontinued Google Glass as a consumer product in 2015 although it continues being used in the workplace today and Google collaborate with other industries wishing to use Google Glass.

Facebook is hard at work on delivering smartglasses that can let you see virtual objects in the real world through its virtual reality subsidiary, Oculus. Facebook CEO Mark Zuckerberg has called virtual and augmented reality the next major computing platform capable of replacing smartphones and traditional PCs (Heath 2017).

Apple has major plans for AR. Apple's brand new ARKit uses the iPhone to create a vast framework of sensors and software so that augmented reality apps can be purchased from Apple's app store and used on the iPhone. A popular example is IKEA's new app. It allows people to stand in their living room and look at a virtual recreation of the sofa they want to buy – then they can check how it fits, move around it, look how it goes with the wallpaper, and so on. Online rumours suggest that Apple AR glasses will be launched in 2019.

The cost of AR has not put off industries who are reaping its benefits. It has been shown to aid in building projects. This was demonstrated publicly when Disney Shanghai China was built. During the design phase, Grimshaw, a British-based firm of architects, created a detailed digital model of 3D visualisations from their 2D drawings that enabled numerous stakeholders to walk through the environment in an immersive virtual space.

In machine plant rooms, where both hands may be needed to operate a system, the information – such as temperature, pressure, speed and status – can be displayed as AR next to each particular section and AR images can be overlaid on equipment, so that you can strip away layers of components to see what lies underneath while you fix that piece of equipment.

It doesn't take much imagination to see how this can and will be applied in hospital operating theatres, in sport and other industries. As artificial intelligence becomes more refined, the challenges for AR use in large scale industrial projects will lessen.

A blind person will never be able to see the holograms in front of them but that doesn't mean they cannot have their reality augmented by digitalisation. Computer vision scientist Professor Philip Torr and neuroscientist Stephen Hicks, founded OxSight[7] in 2016. Both men also work at Oxford University and are leaders in the field of computer vision and augmented reality. The AR OxSight Prism glasses can enhance sight for visually impaired people. They are designed to enhance vision for people with peripheral vision loss caused by conditions such as glaucoma, diabetes, retinitis pigmentosa and other degenerative eye diseases.

Bose is known for its surround sound. It is developing the world's first audio augmented reality glasses. Unlike visual AR, which adds an extra layer of things you can see, Bose AR[8] adds an extra layer of things you can hear. It doesn't display anything in front of your eyes but depends on immersive audio experiences. Using only a Bose AR-equipped wearable and an app enabled with Bose AR, the new platform can speak quietly into your ear to give you reminders and pertinent information on what you see and where you are going, making everything more meaningful. All you provide are simple head movements, voice commands and taps on your wearable – the Bose AR platform does the rest.

Apps with AR

At Great Ormond Street Hospital (GOSH) collaboration with Microsoft has already offered young patients distraction from anxiety with a Gruffalo Augmented Reality app.

Figure 2.6 AR Gruffalo app

What is artificial intelligence (AI)

John McCarthy, a computer scientist, coined the term "artificial intelligence" in 1955. He organised the first Artificial Intelligence conference in 1956. But as with both VR and AR it is only in the past 10 years that there have been rapid advances. Breakthroughs in machine learning algorithms, big data and deep learning are responsible for these advances. To understand AI, we should understand what an algorithm is.

Figure 2.7 AI summit London 2018

Algorithms

An algorithm is a set of steps to accomplish a task. In computer science algorithms, work on problem-solving such tasks as planning a route from home to a holiday destination. This is called a route-finding algorithm. The steps have to be followed by the computer or robot in the right order to get the desired result. A good algorithm has to be correct and efficient. It's similar to a jig[9] we would write in a special school showing a student with autism steps on how to get home. We might do this using symbols, pictures or words as below, dependent upon the learning style of the student.

1. Walk to school bus
2. Get on school bus
3. Sit on school bus seat

4. Arrive at home
5. Get off school bus
6. Walk into house

No wonder our students with autism can relate to computers so well.

Brownies are the section in the Girl Guides organisation aged seven to 10. They now have a badge to earn that is called the digital design badge sponsored by Google. To get the badge they will need to understand how algorithms work and put them into action. Google is also sponsoring the development of a new digital design badge for rangers aged 14–18.

Jaron Lanier (Lanier 2017) recognises, as does Klint Finley, that "todays internet is ruled by algorithms. These mathematical creations determine what you see in your Facebook feed, what movies Netflix recommends to you, and what ads you see in your Gmail" (Finley 2014).

Artificial intelligence is a concept and machine learning is the way to achieve that concept. Deep learning is a subset of machine learning that relies on big data.

Machine learning

Machine learning works by training computer systems to use algorithms to spot patterns in data and then behave in a predictive way. As new data are provided to the machine, the algorithm's performance improves, resulting in increasing machine intelligence over time. Machine learning is where a system can learn things without being programmed to do so. Spam detection is an example of machine learning.

Big data

Big data is a term that describes the large volume of data – both structured and unstructured – that inundates us on a day-to-day basis. The importance of big data doesn't revolve around how much data you have, but what you do with it. Big data can be analysed to enable us to make decisions.

When you are travelling on a plane, do you pay a premium to sit together as a family or did the airline put you together? The algorithm would have determined that you have the same surname. The airline decided how they were going to use that data information.

Data analysis

This is the process of examining, rinsing, transforming and creating data with the goal of discovering useful information and supporting decision-making.

Deep learning

Deep learning handles the large volumes of data and is able to bring the data together. Its performance improves with more data. It uses artificial neural networks similar to how neural networks in the brain process information. These have enabled the recent advances in machine learning. Deep learning is a subset of machine learning, as is data analysis.

Automatic language translation is an example of deep learning and this has enabled the use of AI in the form of chatbots now available on many websites. Xiaoice[10] is a Microsoft bot widely used in China that sings lullabies to children to help them go to sleep and it has even phoned a person to express concern over their health.

Smart

AI is an intelligent system that is computerised and makes decisions or performs tasks that a human would ordinarily carry out. It frees up our time and does mundane processes on our behalf. Examples of current day AI are all of the Smart Home devices that can turn on lights when you enter the home, lock the door for you or play music with one voice command. Spotify is not a smart home device but it could be considered as a form of AI because it uses machine learning to analyse data to find patterns in your playlists' preferences. The song suggestions Spotify give you are based on your personal and also collective customer algorithms.

Google Cloud AI offers schools many aspects of machine learning, including Photos (image search), Translate, Inbox (Smart Reply), and the Google app (voice search) as well as their Vision API that can quickly classify images into thousands of categories, detects individual objects and faces within images, and finds and reads printed words contained within images. Facebook's Computer Vision Engine can do that and more but it is not available to schools.

Microsoft has its own AI platform that offers machine learning and promotes fairness, accountability, transparency and ethical use in the use of AI. Both Facebook and Apple have their own AI research platforms. Amazon Web Services (AWS) provides on-demand cloud computing platforms to individuals, companies and governments. Amazon has its own AI platform called SageMaker.

AI assistants

There are currently four major players competing to be AI assistants in your home: Amazon (Alexa), Apple (Siri), Google (Assistant) and Microsoft (Cortana). These virtual assistants should be able to book you a flight, restaurant or hotel, give you directions, read the news, and make a music play recommendation based on the data they have stored.

Drones

Drones have been, up till now, flying computers with a camera sensor attached. Drone technology is constantly evolving as new innovations and big investments aid its technological improvements. The latest drones could be classed as AI. They are able to use intelligent algorithms and face recognition technology. A drone can now sense obstacles in its path and use diversionary tactics. It will return home if it loses its signal. They are beginning to be used in schools to aid subjects such a geography, geology and environmental sciences. They could even be used to watch over children walking the dog, reporting back to parents with any alerts.

Figure 2.8 Childminding drone

The Turing test

AI systems are good at logical tasks but they're not capable of intuition, empathy or emotional intelligence. Alan Turing came up with a test to determine if a machine was capable of these.

In about 2006 I was asked along to observe the Turing Test taking place at Reading University. It was the annual Loebner Prize competition with a prize of $100,000 (£63,500) to the creator of a machine that could pass the Turing Test. The experiment investigates whether people can detect if they are talking to machines or humans.

If a computer is mistaken for a human more than 30% of the time during a series of five-minute keyboard conversations it passes the test. No computer achieved it on the day I attended and I speculated whether a fairer test would have been a computer versus a person with autism, as on that particular day the judges told me that it was easy to detect the human as computers showed no emotion in their answers.

In 2014, Eugene was one of five computer programmes battling for the Turing Test Prize and it managed to convince 33% of the judges that it was human. Professor Kevin Warwick said on the day:

> In the field of Artificial Intelligence there is no more iconic and controversial milestone than the Turing Test, when a computer convinces a sufficient number of interrogators into believing that it is not a machine but rather is a human.

(www.reading.ac.uk/news-and-events/releases/PR583836.aspx)

Now that AI has crossed that frontier and computers behave more like humans, there is justification to the human fear that AI could take over the world. The lion is mighty and strong but doesn't rule the world. Man does – because of his intelligence. When computers become more intelligent than man, will they take over?

It's important to remember that companies like Facebook, Amazon, Apple, Google and Microsoft are all investing huge amounts of money into the development of AI and so we're progressing rapidly toward more humanlike systems. These companies and many others are trying to ensure AI technologies benefit people and society through best practices and open discussion and have set up the Partnership on AI[11] to help protect the future of mankind.

Notes

1 See item 1 in the Appendix and resources chapter
2 See item 2 in the Appendix and resources chapter
3 See item 3 in the Appendix and resources chapter
4 See item 4 in the Appendix and resources chapter
5 See item 5 in the Appendix and resources chapter
6 See item 6 in the Appendix and resources chapter
7 See item 7 in the Appendix and resources chapter
8 See item 8 in the Appendix and resources chapter
9 See item 9 in the Appendix and resources chapter
10 See item 10 in the Appendix and resources chapter
11 See item 11 in the Appendix and resources chapter

3 | Traditional methods and why they fail

Traditional teaching and learning is all about sitting quietly and listening to the teacher teach. Students are expected to learn by assimilation. Many children with autism are regularly excluded (often illegally) from schools as teachers fail to understand the teaching and learning needs of these children (NAS 2018). On average these students spend 6 hours a day, 5 days a week, 39 weeks a year in school taught in a way that does not engage, inspire or meet their individual learning styles.

It is claimed that after two weeks an *ordinary* person tends to remember:

10% of what they read

20% of what they hear

30% of what they see

50% of what they see and hear

70% of what they say

90% of what they say and do.

In 1974 Piaget wrote *The Future of Education* in which he advises that "Instead of evaluating only from the angle of future scholastic success, in the sense of being a step in the ladder toward only one goal-the university-the school is responsible for discovering and developing the most diverse individual talents" (Piaget 1974, p. 72).

Piaget's recommendation was that the traditional ways of teaching where students were passive recipients of information should cease.

In *Mindstorms* (1980) Seymour Papert, the father of educational computing, wrote "Many children are held back in their learning because they have a model of learning in which you have either 'got it' or 'got it wrong'" (p. 23). But when you program a computer you almost never get it right the first time. Learning to be a master programmer is learning to become highly skilled at isolating and correcting bugs. The question to ask about the program is not whether it is right or wrong, but if it is fixable. If this way of looking at intellectual products were generalised to how the larger culture thinks about knowledge and its acquisition, we might all be less intimidated by our fears of "being wrong".

One of our students, who has Asperger syndrome, used his school iPad to download animation apps. He then scripted and produced a two-minute animated film. Whatever digital fluidity he possessed, it hadn't been taught to him. Creating a short animated film could take hours, and it almost always involves failure that is brief, surmountable, often exciting but not scary. Traditional forms of teaching rarely work for students with Asperger.

Current educational thinking

Marc Prensky believes that an academic education is no longer relevant for the world we live in and he believes that

> If we give our students real world problems to solve in school then we produce a population of adult citizens who have been empowered, by their education, to actually create solutions to real-world problems. Those adults will therefore go on creating real, world-improving solutions for the rest of their lives.
>
> (2016, p. 6)

Around the world today, educational leaders, such as Graham Donaldson, champion the need for education to stimulate minds and consciences, whilst developing personalities.

At the beginning of the twenty-first century, in order to bring education into line with the needs of society, it has been necessary for many countries to undertake a complete revision of the methods and aims of education systems. It is exciting to read of the recommendations that all students will be more actively involved in their own learning and that constructivist teachers will replace the more traditional and conservative teachers.

In 1974 Piaget recommended a reorganisation of education including specialised training and professional development of teachers in order to bring about changes in education to meet with the recommendations of Article 26 in the Universal Declaration of Human Rights. This seems, at first glance, no different from Donaldson's recommendations in *Successful Futures* (2015).

New technology supports the current educational thinking that students are better able to master, retain and generalise new knowledge when they are actively involved in constructing that knowledge in a learning-by-doing situation. The flipped classroom is a new and popular approach that makes the student an active participant in the acquisition of knowledge. The maker movement is a movement that exploded in popularity in America in recent years. The maker culture emphasises learning-through-doing and is hugely popular both in schools and with the general public. In both instances teachers have found themselves acting as facilitators who support students in these educational approaches.

In Australia, Natalie Richie (2017) reported that a middle schooler created an app for younger students so that they could reserve seats in the school café at lunch time to stop them being bullied. She added that in another school a student created an app that listens for sounds of domestic violence and when it hears them calls the police. These instances hark back to Marc Prensky's suggestion that problem solving is the future of education. Not class or school based problem solving but actual real world problem solving empowering students because they have made a positive difference to the world they live in.

A study financed by the Bill and Melinda Gates Foundation (2006) set out to examine the reasons that almost a third of American public-high-school students fail to graduate with their class. Researchers surveyed high-school dropouts in 25 cities, suburbs and small towns across the country, where they were consistently told that school was boring. The final report recommended, among other things, that educators take steps to 'make school more relevant and engaging'. Governments across the world are attempting to do that.

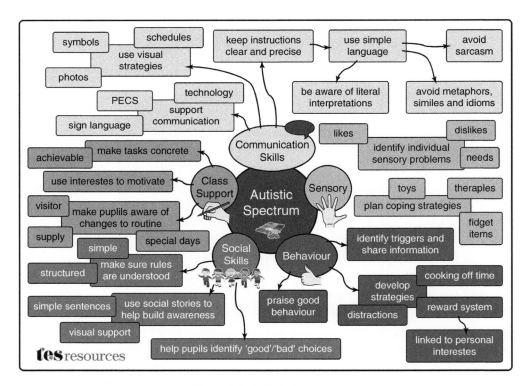

Figure 3.1 Autistic Spectrum
Adapted from from TES resources (www.tes.com)

The Institute for Play[1] is part of a small but increasingly influential group of education specialists who believe that school should be about preparing students for the world in which we now live, an exponential digitally mediated world.

Paul Howard-Jones, a neuroscientist who teaches in the graduate school of education at the University of Bristol in Britain is quoted as saying: "I think in 30 years' time we will marvel that we ever tried to deliver a curriculum without gaming". Whilst E. O. Wilson, the renowned Harvard evolutionary biologist said in an interview with the game designer Will Wright "I think games are the future in education. We're going through a rapid transition now. We're about to leave print and textbooks behind" (Corbett 2010).

One can only hope that each of us will be able to look back to the beginning of the twenty-first century as the time when educational change was no longer just written about but it actually happened.

And what of those students who are not ordinary? After two weeks what do they remember? If a child can't learn the way we teach, maybe we should teach the way they learn.

Multiple intelligences

The education system has focussed in the past on weaknesses instead of strengths and in correcting those weaknesses. Harvard psychologist Howard Gardner identified that students possess different kinds of minds and therefore learn, remember, perform, and understand in different ways (Gardner 1993). This is obvious to many of us who work with students in the field of education. If we look at how Gardner's theory of multiple intelligences has evolved amongst educationalists over the years we can use that information to identify the strengths of individual students and also get them to identify what they perceive as their strengths. We can then focus on these strengths to provide a better, more appropriate education.

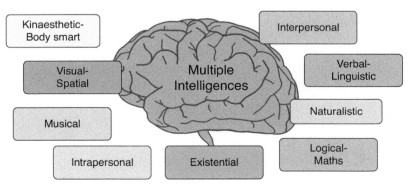

Figure 3.2 Multiple Intelligences
© The author

This is particularly important when working with students who are classed as having a learning disability or difficulty. If, like me, you embrace the concept of neurodiversity and believe that people with differences do not need to be cured but need a different way of teaching and support.

I have been particularly excited this year by the work staff in our school have done to give our students the opportunity to develop their skills through their strengths and interests with the support of the latest technology.

The process of writing

Many children with learning difficulties have struggled with the process of writing. They may have dyspraxia or fine motor skill (FMS) problems. One of my pet hates as a special school head teacher would be to walk into a class where the teacher was encouraging children, who find writing difficult, to trace over sentences or copy write their "News". Why would anyone make someone do something repeatedly that that someone finds difficult or maybe impossible to do?

I remember doing an observation at a school as an Estyn peer inspector a number of years ago where a staff member returned an ambulant child to a postural support chair, strapped him in and hand over hand copied over letters on a worksheet. When I asked why that was done I was told it was evidence for the teacher that he had done some "work". Thankfully I have never encountered that approach to education since.

According to a 2017 report by Ofcom, 39% of 8–11-year-olds own a smartphone, while 52% of 8 to 11-year-olds own a tablet (Ofcom 2017).

More and more parents are ensuring that their children have their own iPads and their homes are awash with the latest technological aids where a child can even tell *Alexa* to play the top 10 Nursery rhymes. These children are digital savvy and expect to use technology in school.

I was therefore very surprised when babysitting an ordinary six-year-old mainstream child over the Christmas period to find that their mainstream school, in a leafy London suburb, still relies on the pen and paper method.

The child was bursting with ideas for a story and was thrilled to be shown how to use a keyboard and a word processing programme that even suggested possible words. She proceeded to write and edit a little book and was thrilled with what she had achieved. I asked her how she wrote stories in school and if her class had iPads. She told me that they were not allowed to take iPads to school, did not have iPads in class and had "word books" to aid writing.

Teachers need, if possible to ensure that students from nursery age upwards are computationally literate because that is the way society communicates now. They will be writing blogs online instead of writing their "news" as soon as they are shown how to do it. We need to educate them in online writing because we cannot remain blinkered to the fact that as soon as many students get home from school they go online to download a game or an app or go on social media.

It is important that we show students how to collaborate online with school-based projects so that the internet is regarded as a tool for learning. We need to transform their passion for social networking and gaming into productive learning experiences.

Handwriting is a skill but it is no longer the primary skill needed in order to write.

As adults do we use pen and paper on a daily basis or do we use the keyboard? If we want our children and grandchildren to keep pace with the real-world then what skills should we be teaching our students? Do we really wish to stunt creativity? The technology evolution may seem daunting but we educators should all ensure that the classroom experience inspires every child to realise their full potential because we have a new generation of learners. These learners need to be taught how to use the internet because the pen is no longer mightier than the sword. It has been superceded by the keyboard.

All of the students at our school have individualised iPads to meet their educational needs. They are updated regularly to ensure they correspond to the learning needs of the individual student. Some students choose to take their iPads into the hall at lunchtime to assist them in selecting lunch. I sat with one such student recently who had finished his lunch and had chosen to write a story using a word processing app on his iPad. He has autism and before he had his iPad staff would have been trying to find something to keep him occupied and happy while he waited for the end of lunch bell to sound.

The majority of our students have fine motor skill problems and use both a keyboard skills app and a word processing app that enables them to *write* using the latest technology. We also have BigKeys keyboards for our computers as the usual keyboard keys are too small for a lot of our pupils.

Our students who are able, may practice tracing over or copying their name, as it is something they may need to write when they leave education but technology may soon negate that necessity. I believe handwriting is a twentieth century skill and in this day and age it makes sense for all children to be encouraged to learn keyboard and word processing skills.

Dictation

For those students who suffer with dyslexia or feel that typing or writing still doesn't match their pace of thought then technology still has the answer. With Dragon Naturally Speaking software you can also use your voice to dictate documents or enter text anywhere you normally type. Dragon eliminates barriers to productivity and creativity by letting you interact with your computer by voice. It turns your spoken thoughts into text and your voice commands into action so you don't have to worry about the mechanics of typing and spelling. How many schools that have students with dyslexia have access to this kind of software I wonder? Microsoft also provide free support for the struggling reader with a programme called Immersive Reader.

What other strengths do these students have that could be nurtured? It was no surprise to me in 2013 when the then Lord Chancellor and Secretary of State for Justice the Rt. Hon. Chris Grayling (2013) stated that

> young offenders in prison are ten times more likely to have learning disabilities (23–32% v 2–4%) and a high proportion of them – maybe more than half – will have dyslexia (43–57%). That compares with just 10 percent in the population as a whole.

Reading

We have had interactive whiteboards supporting the reading scheme *Oxford Reading Tree* since we opened in 2009. We find that students with autism, on the whole, do not like their space being invaded by sitting right next to them as they read aloud from an ordinary book or a Kindle. Often they choose not to read aloud and it can be difficult to tell if they are able to read. Reading tests can be misleading.

We have found that the use of the white board for teaching and supporting reading to be invaluable. Sometimes students like to be on the periphary of a lesson observing what is on the white board and appear not to be taking part. On occasion I have heard students repeat parts of the story they didn't appear to be taking notice of.

I recall my niece who was having problems with exams study relating to Shakespeare's Romeo and Juliet some years ago. I took her to see the ballet and it is a memory she treasures to this day. She told me it brought the story alive. Today virtual reality can take you to the ballet without having to leave the classroom. This is ideal for students with autism who may find it difficult entering a theatre but are struggling with study skills.

iBooks and Kindles can now read aloud to students so that students can hear the story repeatedly before they try to learn to read it. Whatever works to encourage a reluctant reader is worth trying.

It may seem daunting to a newly qualified teacher to teach to all learning styles. However, as we move into the fourth industrial revolution it becomes easier. As we understand learning styles, it becomes apparent why certain technologies appeal to learners and why certain technologies are effective in supporting learning. AI support in classes will become the norm.

The SAMR model

The **S**ubstitution **A**ugmentation **M**odification **R**edefinition (SAMR) model below is the brainchild of Dr. Ruben Puentedura. It can be used to make technology integration smoother for teachers and their classes. It allows teachers to see how technology can completely transform teaching and it gives students the opportunity to work collaboratively with other students with minimal guidance from the teacher. It is a very useful tool for all teachers to have in their tool box. Some of our students with autism are already on the redefinition stage for some projects that interest them.

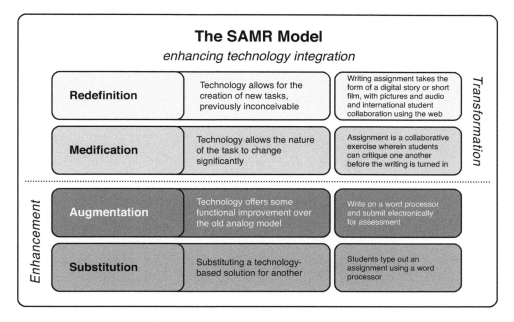

Figure 3.3 The SAMR model
devised by R.R Puentedura, Ph.D, adapted by author

The Padagogy Wheel

Teachers can also access a reference tool that ties apps to specific learning outcomes directly connected to modern pedagogies and theories. It is called the Padagogy Wheel. All around the world universities are using it as an integral part of initial teacher training to encourage research and methodology in e-learning, distance education and the use of technologies in education.

Teachers can easily sit with the wheel during lesson planning time to find tools that will best aid their students. Or use it during class time to extend or deepen learning towards a specific twenty-first century skill or content area.

The Padagogy Wheel was based on Blooms taxonomy, thought by many to be the backbone of modern teaching. Andrew Churches produces some amazing work in relation to Blooms taxonomy. I like his infographic that links Blooms Digital Taxonomy to the communication spectrum.[2]

Apps for Students with Autism Spectrum Disorders

When looking for apps for students on the autism spectrum (ASD), it is important to look at all educational apps and not just those that are tagged as autism apps. They have many of the same learning needs that other students have. This list was developed to provide apps based on common learning characteristics and traits that are typical for students with ASD. It is important to remember that all students learn differently and selecting apps should be based on the unique learning needs of the student.

This list is only a sampling of apps available for each skill area. This is not, nor is it meant to be a definitive list. This list is intended to give you a starting place and a rationale for picking certain apps.

○ Common Learning Characteristics

◐ Common Learning Traits

● App Categories

○ Apps

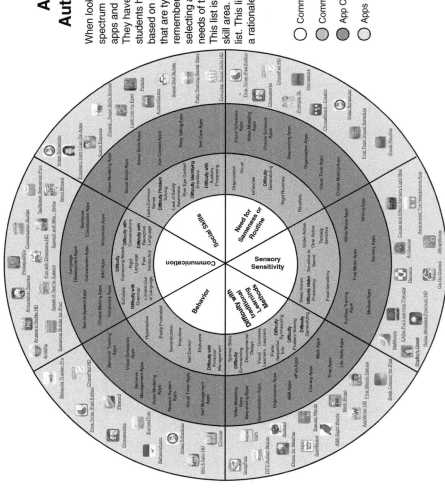

Figure 3.4 Padagogy wheel for Autism

Design based on the Padagogy Wheel, adapted from model designed by Alan Carrington and modified by Cherie Pickering, available at: www.autismspeaks.org/sites/default/files/pedagogy_wheel.pdf

Alan Carrington has connected apps to the taxonomy. Version 1 in 2012 was 62 iPad apps categorised according to Blooms cognitive domain and was useful to lots of teachers. It evolved to version 2 with additions and so on until we are now at version 5. At this time of writing it has been translated into 19 different languages. The core of the Padagogy Wheel is all about excellent teaching and how we get the best out of the technology (SAMR). Below is a YouTube link on how to use a version of the wheel: www. youtube.com/watch?v=RAYVQlUVpK4

Versions have already been adapted at universities for a padagogy wheel to meet all kinds of needs. Please follow the link below to view an app wheel describing apps useful to those with autistic spectrum disorders.

iPad apps for *complex communication support* can be downloaded from http://bit.ly/ CALL-AAC-App-Wheel

In the electronic version, app names are 'clickable' links, taking you to information about the individual app on the iTunes site for the UK.

iPad apps for *dyslexia support* can be downloaded from www.callscotland.org.uk/ downloads/posters-and-leaflets

Tech giants

Twenty-first century teaching extends beyond the role of teacher instruction to facilitator of learning. A facilitator of learning guided and supported by technological innovations.

Tech giants Microsoft, Google, Apple, Amazon and even Facebook are leading the way in assisting schools' implementation of these new forms of technology for free. It is hardly surprising given the billions that these companies have invested in AR/VR and AI. Students in schools will potentially later become customers of these industries perhaps throughout their lifetime. As well as developing the use of VR/AR and AI in schools the giants support schools in other ways for free (CNBC 2017).

Microsoft provides free learning tools for reading that reduce visual crowding, enable text highlighting and voicing and break words into syllables as well as parts of speech; a picture dictionary is included in their support package. Microsoft provides writing support with tools like Dictation and Read Aloud. Using these tools students can hear their writing read aloud so that they can edit it. Learning support tools are already available to all users of Word, One Note, Outlook and Microsoft Edge. Students and teachers are eligible for Office 365 Education for free, which includes Word, Excel, PowerPoint, One Note, Microsoft Teams plus additional classroom tools. Microsoft has also joined partners with LEGO® Education and provide tutorials, projects and code samples to help schools get started using Microsoft MakeCode for *LEGO MINDSTORMS* Education EV3.

Google for Education provides G suite and Google Classroom for free to schools. It provides free tools to help teachers manage their classrooms with assignment distribution, quizzes, giving feedback and tracking student progress. It allows student collaboration on documents, reminds you of tasks to do and supports video conferencing. It lets teachers work one to one with students on a document or with the whole class. The *Times Educational Supplement* (TES) hosts lesson ideas and teacher materials designed by the global Google for Education community. Teachers can become a Google Certified Educator and broadcast practice-based ideas, tools and tips to a worldwide network of teachers as a member of the TES community.

Apple Teacher is a free online programme to help teachers build their skills in using Apple products effectively as learning tools. You can earn the official Apple Teacher logo. Apple provide many free apps on its app store for schools. Apple reduce the costs of many of their products if you inform them that you are purchasing for a school. If you sign up for their school manager account, your school gets 50% discount on most apps. Students can also get discount on products.

Facebook Education is a Facebook page for the professional learning community to come together, to share, learn and inspire. It hosts events, shares resources and engages the educational community in global events. Facebook have also worked with individual public schools on personalised learning.

Amazon is newer to the education market and offers a cloud-based storage, data, and analytics system through its Amazon Web Services. The system can replace physical storage. Amazon also have an educational platform called Amazon Inspire which is an open-source curriculum tool to find new, vetted materials and lessons.

There are other online education platforms with varying degrees of support and a search online will show platforms you may wish to follow up.

Teaching and learning in schools needs to change and it needs to change now. We need to embrace technology with collaborative online learning projects and more game- approach teaching styles because this is what our tech savvy students are doing easily outside of school. We do a disservice to them by labelling them as having learning difficulties when they can easily win games on their play stations and communicate on social media platforms.

For those students with more severe needs technology is already providing some exciting possibilities as this book will show.

Notes

1 See item 5 in the Appendix and resources chapter
2 See item 12 in the Appendix and resources chapter

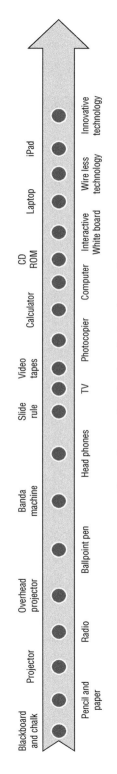

Figure 3.5 *The Evolution of Technology for Teaching and Learning*

The pathways to teaching and learning using our senses

4

In 350BC Aristotle was confident that there were no more senses than those of sight, hearing, touch, taste and smell. Bruce Durie used some practical experiments to demonstrate how implausible it is to still believe in just five senses (Durie 2005).

We now know that we have receptors all over our bodies that pick up sensory information, or 'stimuli'. Some scientists believe we have up to 21 senses. Educators today are familiar with both the vestibular sense – the sense of balance, and the proprioceptive sense – the sense of spatial awareness. The names of other more-subtle senses don't trip off the end of the tongue as easily. Neuron receptors sense movement to control balance and the tilt of the head. Specific kinaesthetic receptors exist for detecting stretching in muscles and tendons, helping people to keep track of their limbs. Other receptors detect levels of oxygen in certain arteries of the bloodstream.

Today as we look towards person-centred planning for all children in all schools we are looking to provide a curriculum that takes account of all students sensory needs as well as their strengths and preferences in order for them to get the very best education possible. However, a disability may limit the type of information a student may access, and in fact, the disability may even conflict with the student's preferred modality.

Many children with autism have difficulty with multiple sources of sensory input (Grandin and Scariano 1996). A high percentage of the students at our school experience sensory processing difficulties. Students with sensory input deficiency may be over-sensitive (hypersensitive) in some or all senses. Conversely, other students may be under-sensitive (hyposensitive) in some or all senses. This means individuals are often over (hyper) or under (hypo) sensitive to visual, auditory, olfactory, oral, vestibular or proprioceptive stimuli. This varies for student to student- some experience difficulties in processing all of the senses, some experience no difficulties at all.

There is also a wide spectrum of sensory, multi-sensory and physical difficulties. The sensory range extends from profound and permanent deafness or visual defect through to lesser levels of loss, which may not be permanent. Physical difficulties may arise from physical, neurological or metabolic causes.

Anyone working in a school needs to be aware that every interaction they have with a student is sensory, all material things in the school setting are sensory, and every person in the school is sensory, and so concepts like "sensory stimulation" or "sensory time" or "sensory materials" are misleading (Brown 2012).

Special schools are committed to assisting students to achieve their potential, both cognitively and emotionally and supporting them through providing a multi-sensory environment in which their individual learning styles are paramount to teaching. The physical and emotional well-being of all students is the foundation for their ability to make sense of the cognitive demands of the educational curriculum.

Special schools today have moved forward from the tendency to offer a 'sensory curriculum' to students who were considered not yet ready to access the regular curriculum. Sometimes staff working with these students would have had very little understanding of individual needs and how a "sensory curriculum" could be made educational.

Assistive technology has advanced exponentially in recent years to support teaching and learning through more strategic use of the senses. It is a very exciting time for assisting students with communication difficulties.

The highest bandwidth inbound sensory pathway to the brain comes from the eyes via the optic nerve. It makes sense that technology has been developed to exploit that fact.

Figure 4.1 The eye

Eye Gaze is an artificial intelligence-based electrical machine that allows students with limited speech or hand movements to communicate. More information can be found in the chapter on AI.

A lot of our students are visual learners and we use visual cues in its many forms to support them. We have a member of staff trained in the use of Irlen lens that may support students with reading problems or suffering with eye-strain, headaches, or migraines.

It is also worth bearing in mind that some students have a sensitivity to visual stimuli. They may see incredible detail in everything or they may find bright lights painful, and patterns on clothing or furnishings can be distracting to the point of causing nausea. Teachers can support children by ensuring environments are uncluttered, plain and not too brightly lit to minimise unwanted visual stimuli.

Figure 4.2 The ear

The auditory learning style is the kind of learning in which a learner absorbs information much better by way of hearing. A student is more comfortable with listening to audio books, enjoying music therapy and using listening stations to access podcasts and other audio materials. The teacher will need to decide where it is best for the student to work to avoid distractions and concentrate more on what information needs to be processed.

Some students may have auditory processing disorder. A child's auditory system isn't fully developed until the age of 15. The support of a speech therapist and the use of computer-assisted programs that help the brain do a better job of processing sounds in a noisy environment can work wonders.

Some students may find certain noises, or loud noises, distracting or painful. Background noise can be overwhelming and it can be difficult to focus on the lesson. We have found ear defenders useful and they are now widely available.

Provision for the Deaf and Hearing Impaired in schools include regular visits by a Speech and Language Therapist, a deaf signing instructor and a tutor. The continued merging of electronic innovation and hearing aid technology mean hearing aids are becoming smaller, sleeker and smarter. Different degrees and types of hearing loss, as well as differences in a patient's ability to use the technology, will have an impact on the results but technological progress has allowed users many practical benefits like wireless connectivity via Bluetooth.

Today audio quality listening environment and sound field systems are often installed in the classrooms where the hearing impaired students work as well as the hall. Access to the curriculum is through oral methods, BSL and sign-supported English. Students are usually encouraged to develop good listening, lip-reading and speaking skills as well.

The highest bandwidth outbound pathway to a single organ goes to the tongue. BrainPort® is an intra-oral device that uses the tongue because it is more sensitive and a better electrical conductor than other areas of the body. Brainport®, it is claimed, can compensate for lost eyesight, improve your balance and a range of vestibular disorders. Brainport® is not yet ready to be used in schools. Speech and language therapy is delivered daily in many special schools.

Figure 4.3 Tongue

Smelling is much more than the simple detection of odours in the surrounding environment. It has unique properties linked to memories and emotions contained in the brain. We use aromatherapy diffusers throughout the school and many students recognise the daily aromas. Our VR room can offer a nebulising aroma delivery system allowing instant access to a wide selection of scents that complete the multi-sensory experience. Aromas can soothe and calm the mind, create a positive sense of well-being and stimulate the imagination. We have access to over 400 pressurised aromas for use in the VR room.

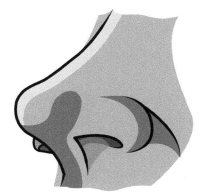

Figure 4.4 Nose

The term *haptic* covers the sensations that are felt through the spinal cord. It includes touch, feel and how the body senses its shape and motion (proprioception). It is how you feel whether a surface is hot or cold etc. Tactile sensation is an aspect of haptics. A blind student passes fingers over Braille and increases the size of their somatosensory cortex because of repeated use of the sense of touch applied. Though the experience may not be exactly like seeing words, the blind student has read those words using a different modality. The brain figures out how to use the sensory signals it takes in because of its plasticity. We know this because advances in technology allow us to view the human brain at work. Haptics offers an additional dimension to both AR

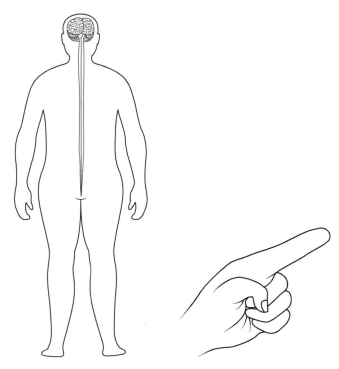

Figure 4.5 Haptic senses through spine and hands

and VR technology and is essential to the immersiveness of and interaction with those environments.

Touch therapies such as TACPAC® Story Massage® Vibroacoustic therapy and Reflexology have been very successful for many of our students. It is extremely reward-ing to be able to provide our students with these therapies which have proven to make a positive impact not only on the physical and emotional well-being of our students but also in supporting each to achieve their educational targets. Helping students to be in the right frame of mind to learn to achieve their potential is the very cornerstone of providing therapies in a special school.

The Sunu band is a form of new technology that will aid blind and partially sighted students. It is a bracelet that uses ultrasonic sonar technology to detect the user's sur-roundings and send haptic feedback whenever an obstacle comes into proximity. This technology uses a combination of augmented reality and radar.

Sensory Circuits

Our school offers a sensory circuit to students with a sensory processing disorder. Sensory circuits involve three types of activities; when used in order they can be effective in

Figure 4.6 Sensory Circuit

supporting individuals to improve their levels of attention and focus in the classroom. Opportunities to move and participate in 10–15 minute sessions will allow students to improve their brain processing efficiency and engage them making them ready to learn and participate. Circuits are organised into three main sections:

- *Alerting* To provided vestibular stimulation -activities that make the head change direction rapidly e.g. bouncing, jumping, skipping, step ups and spinning.

- *Organising* The second set of activities require multi-sensory processing and balance. They should provide motor challenges to the child.

- *Calming* The third set of activities should be those that calm the child such as deep pressure, proprioceptive input and heavy work. It is very important to provide input that ensures that as a student leaves the circuit and enters the classroom they are as calm and centred as possible.

Sensory circuits are highly effective for students with sensory processing problems and can help them to regulate their sensory needs. Schools can set up their own sensory circuits using equipment that they possibly already have in their PE store.

While it is relatively easy to assess a student's preferred style of learning, identifying and then teaching preferentially to a particular modality at the exclusion of others is difficult at best when you consider the different learning styles within a class. It will however be possible in a few years' time when artificial intelligence (AI) is available for use in all classrooms so that each student has their own personal assistant who has been programmed to meet their individual needs and most effective learning styles.

Whilst students with learning difficulties could struggle with technology requiring high levels of cognitive competence it is reassuring to note that technological advances can also allow those students access to educational opportunities unavailable to them in the past.

Note

1 See item 13 in the Appendix and resources chapter

Virtual reality (VR)

Teaching and learning opportunities for students with learning difficulties

We are living in exponential times. In the near future children will be using technologies that haven't even been invented yet.

I believe that in the next decade virtual reality, more commonly referred to as VR, will make a huge difference to special education as we know it. It can facilitate learning through stimulating more of the senses than traditional teaching has done up to now. We are on the cusp of a serious and arguably revolutionary step in technology provision that schools who have students with learning disabilities need to take seriously as a classroom resource.

Imagine being able to transport students with learning difficulties who also happen to be in wheelchairs to anywhere in the world without having to leave the classroom. Do you think your students might have dreamed of visiting Disneyland and experiencing rides never thought possible? Have they ever wanted to swim with dolphins?

On a more academic level, have you ever wanted your students to really see what a volcano is like when you are teaching them about volcanoes? It wouldn't necessarily be very safe or within budget to give your students first-hand experience. It is now possible for them to experience a Super volcano in Yellowstone National Park in America through the power of VR. Instead of trying to get visual learners to understand how the body functions they can now travel through the human body to learn about it.

Virtual reality makes all of this possible.

It is possible and important to embed VR into schemes of work and incorporate into areas of the curriculum so that the impact of its use isn't damaged by ignorance. It should be planned and used as a learning tool. It is also possible to use VR to aid student mental health.

Children with learning disabilities can have phobias and fears about real life situations. It is important for parents and teachers to know how to prepare students with a learning disability for those situations.

Often students with learning difficulties have to overcome barriers to learning such as emotional turmoil. How often has a parent of a young child with autism stood by helplessly as their child has a meltdown in a supermarket, at a road crossing, on a train? How can we use technology to make real life situations easier for children with autism?

Children with autism have been shown to display high levels of comfort with technology for many reasons. Those of us who work with children who have autism know how much they like computers, iPads and other kinds of technology. Computer programmes are predictable, logical, and can provide an intellectual outlet for children with specialised interests. This age of technological advancements has come at a serendipitous time for children with autism.

We have found that virtual reality can help reduce anxieties and prepare students for real life situations that they fear the most. The immersive room experience is very real. It allows students to experience and play out difficult situations that they often meet during their daily life. VR allows a student to explore and experience situations as if they were actually present in that environment or place.

We have found that students who experience virtual reality are able to carry out specific activities with significantly increased confidence. We have found the impact of virtual reality on students' ability to cope when in a fight or flight situation have led to real-life functional improvements for activities that were previously not possible. This has had a significant impact on students' readiness to learn, their wellbeing and engagement. Sometimes the impact is qualitative and sometimes it is quantitative. Learning is qualitatively and quantitatively better if learners are given the opportunity to immerse in the situation they are trying to understand and learn from.

Parents and teachers have watched children with autism play back a scene in a movie over and over again to help them make sense of a confusing world. What if we use that knowledge to recreate virtual reality situations – the local supermarket, the local road crossing, the local train station? What if we have a room that children with autism can enter, press a switch and the room becomes an immersive 360° room with an interactive version of the local crossing.

Safe and secure with a trusted teaching assistant the student can play back that scene/scenes as many times as they wish until they feel comfortable enough to visit its real counterpart.

"Children with autism rarely have opportunities to experience or to learn to cope with day-to-day situations. Using virtual simulations enables them to acquire skills that will make it possible for them to become independent" (Josman and Weiss 2008).

In September 2016 a Therapeutic Virtual Reality room was set up in our school, Ysgol Pen Coch, in North Wales. It gives students a 360° experience. Virtual reality is by its very nature a visual oriented experience. Many of our students are thought to be visual learners.

The setting up of this room has enabled us to be able to offer our students the chance to experience and play out difficult situations which they often meet during their daily life and routine. Equipped with floor-to-ceiling screens displaying projected video footage, as well as surround sound, lighting and interactive walls, the room engages students in a complete sensory experience and gives students a feeling of total immersion. The room almost completely filters out interference from outside the room thus allowing the student to focus entirely on the virtual environment.

Handheld controllers and sensors, give a whole new feel to the artificial reality experience. We have transmitters and receivers on the walls and the immersive experience is very real. This is not simply an engagement tool or a gimmick, it allows a student to explore and to experience as if they are actually present in that environment or place.

The experiential situations they can experience were chosen as a result of communicating with parents about situations which caused them the greatest concern. We sent a questionnaire out to our parents asking them what simulations they wanted in the virtual reality room. They gave us a list:

at the hairdressers

crossing the road

going into a forest

being in a crowd

going to the cinema

catching a plane, bus and train

eating at a restaurant

going into a shop or supermarket

The Friends of Ysgol Pen Coch, the school's parent's association, raised the funds for us to have an immersive room put in school during the summer recess of 2016.

For the first trial we used the idea of crossing the road already refined by the university of Haifa. Researchers Professor Naomi Josman and Professor Tamar Weiss, from the university of Haifa in Israel, found that a month-long program of virtual reality training designed locally could help students with autism, aged between seven and 12, dramatically improve their ability to cross the road safely.

It is widely recognised that the best way to teach children with autism is through repeated practice in natural settings. The dangers involved in crossing a street, however, rule this method out. Virtual reality is a good alternative.

A study by The University of Texas at Dallas in the US shows that virtual reality training programmes produce positive results: "The virtual reality training platform creates a safe place for participants to practice social situations without the intense fear of consequence" (Didehbani 2016).

Six autistic students were involved in the study at Haifa university. The children spent a month practicing to cross virtual streets, wait for a virtual light at the crossroads to change, and to look left and right for virtual cars.

The children quickly mastered the different levels of the virtual reality system, including the ninth – most difficult level – where vehicles travel at high speed. They then applied their virtual skills to a local practice area where they were able to navigate a street, crossing and traffic signals. In testing, the researchers found the children showed an improvement in their skills following the training on the virtual street. Three children were found to show considerable improvement.

Our students with learning difficulties often experience difficulty when they are required to wait at the local pedestrian crossing for the three minutes whilst out on an educational visit in the community and as a trial run our first virtual experience that was set up was called "Crossing the Road".

One of our teaching staff visited the local pedestrian crossing and took various photographs and made a recording of all the sounds experienced there. She then transferred these onto a programme on the computer which is connected to the immersive equipment thus creating a VR experience. This resulted in a 3D version of the crossing and relevant sounds being projected onto three walls in the room.

A panorama of the junction is projected on three walls. The coloured spots on the floor are beams of light projected from the ceiling. Each has an image attached, along with an accompanying sound where relevant. These are activated by passing a disc or wand across the appropriate colour to break the beam.

Each student who it was felt would benefit from this extra interaction was offered an individual session of between 10–15 minutes in length once a week spanning over a period of eight weeks in total and split up into three stages. During this time each student was encouraged to act out "crossing the road".

Figure 5.1 Virtual reality room projection

They were required to look for and listen to all the sights and sounds associated with what happens when crossing the road using the pedestrian crossing. They learnt how to press the button to activate the green and red man and they learnt to be patient and wait until it was safe to cross.

Once the children were confident with the first stage of the experience they moved onto the second stage still in the virtual reality room.

Using a timer built into the traffic lights the time lapse was set at exactly the same time as the local crossing. The sequence was worked through and the student was encouraged to wait at the crossing until the lights changed and the green man showed instructing them to cross the road.

At the third stage, students were taken to the actual crossing to see whether the extra input throughout these sessions had been successful or not in helping them cross the road in a safe manner. During a total of one week each small group of students were taken to the "crossing" where the success or failure of the programme was observed.

The results were that out of 30 students who took part in this therapy, all 30 of them were able to arrive at the road crossing, press the button to activate the red and green man and wait patiently until it was time to cross – without becoming agitated or stressed. Each child was able to cross the road with confidence. Each individual session was written up and recorded along with photographs taken of each child experiencing the real crossing.

Figure 5.2 Assessing impact of VR

The virtual reality room has since been used for an individual student whose parents had to do a two- mile detour every day to bring him to school so that they didn't have to go through traffic lights. He was very agitated in the car and screamed if they came upon a traffic light during a car ride. The situation was re-created in the virtual reality room and the student was able to operate the traffic lights for himself. After two weeks of daily visits to the room the parents were able to report that they no longer had to avoid traffic lights. Their child no longer has an issue with traffic lights and was perfectly content in the car. An added bonus was that they could leave home at a reasonable time.

Helen's instructions on how to set up and use a virtual reality room

1. Install an interactive projection system.

2. Buy in training on how to load and operate the system; how to import images, videos and sounds; how to create apps.

3. Send a questionnaire to parents asking them which situation outside of school causes their children the most concern.

4. Photograph the situation using a panoramic setting on a camera or iPhone 7 camera (this is currently the best). Remember always get permission to take photographs where necessary, e.g. Asda.

5. Reproduce the image onto the interactive wall projection.

6. To operate the system, turn on the projectors using the suppliers remote. Four different colours will now be projected onto the floor. Each picture or sound will have been connected to these during the reproduction of the image onto the system.

7. Switch on the system on the computer tower hold the button in and wait until the on light turns blue.

8. The start-up image will appear on three walls in the VR room. Wait until all three walls display this.

9. Use the large remote and when asked press the START button.

10. Scroll through the main subjects using the GROUP until you come to the group you require.

11. Within the group you will have set up individual scenarios. Scroll to the scenario you require using the NEXT button. It is now displayed over three walls and ready to use with your students.

12. The students can now use the given wands to activate the different coloured lights and see the image or hear the sounds chosen.

13. When you wish to close the system down press the power button on the projector remote. You will be asked if you wish to "power off"; press yes and the projectors will shut down.

14. Hold the button in on the tower (same button as is used to start up).

15. Wait until the on light turns white and goes completely out. The system has now shut down.

In the summer term the virtual reality room can also become the school and site of the secondary school that the majority of our Year 6 students transfer to in the following September.

Some of our students were not able to take part in the joint projects planned due to the high anxiety levels they encountered when they attempted to take part in the real-world projects. VR allows for social interactions without the high levels of stress that is commonly encountered in face-to-face exchanges. Thanks to the technology we now have we were able to create a safe in-house virtual reality transition project using repeated practice in allowing those students to get used to the secondary school, its staff and its grounds set up in the VR room in preparation for their actual visits at the end of the summer term.

I visited the secondary school on the first planned transition day, 12 June 2017, and was able to witness every student settled into their transition experience. This continued, without hiccup so that in the September the head teacher reported a 100% successful start for all of our students. This summer is equally successful thanks to the use of the VR room.

The use of virtual reality to create a controlled and safe environment that is closely representative of real life has proven beneficial to students in our care. We all learn by seeing and watching. Students who suffer with fears and phobias are now able to build their own private secure library of how to cope with social situations ordinary students take for granted. VR is proving to be an effective tool for us in enhancing social skills and social cognition in students with autism.

We have also found the VR room ideal for those students with physical disabilities providing them with the opportunity to experience things they may not be able to physically access. Our VR room has enabled us to present information such as video footage, 360° panoramic views of places such as the airport, the dentist, the supermarket, their future secondary school, the local area and further afield.

It enables them to travel to places they might never have gone to, and the room can immerse them in experiences they might never have had otherwise all within the safety of the school walls.

We have found that most of our students do not like wearing the virtual reality glasses that need to be worn by students to give a uniquely personal experience. VR glasses have now become available that students can hold in front of their eyes and we purchased a RedBox 8 box, all-in-one, VR kit for our school. Redbox are partnered with Google Expedition and so our students can take part in immersive field trips all over the world visiting historical landmarks and geographical wonders. At the moment there are over 800 Google expeditions available and this is increasing day by day The package includes eight headsets housed in a bespoke storage and charging case, a teacher's tablet together with links to free lesson plans. No internet connection is needed. The teacher can download the expedition before the lesson and the expedition is then automatically loaded onto the student VR devices.

Google came up with Google Expeditions when they were asked by teachers if they could bring abstract concepts to life. Google expedition can take students on school trips where no bus can go. It is sometimes difficult in a special school to give students an idea of what history is. Students like to dress up in period costumes but now students can individually visit a virtual world to develop an understanding of different periods in history.

The teacher is able to use the teacher tablet to guide the class and tailor the expeditions to the curriculum objectives. Google Expeditions should not be used without proper planning in place. Google expedition is great for those students who can't read textbooks.

Once a school purchases such a set, RedBox will send out a trainer to train a number of staff in its use. The school will need to sign up to G suite and it is free to schools. Redbox will set it up on your behalf if you wish. Six of us were trained by RedBox. Four of those trained then did a presentation to the rest of the teachers, HLTAs and teaching assistants in school. The training of using the VR headsets and teacher's Android teaching device took about 10 minutes. The teaching tablet controls the VR headsets, selects the expedition and can annotate the tablet to direct students. We purchased a set of eight VR headsets for students but you can purchase larger sets. The sets are pre-configured with Google Expeditions and come in a protective charging case with wheels. The 5Ghz router that we have allows us up to 50 users at one time and the expeditions can be downloaded from an app store onto iPad or tablets but there will not be the immersive experience for those students. They can also be transferred onto a class white board to be discussed by the whole class.

The training on using the high resolution 360° Ricoh Theta camera took 15 minutes. It has spherical still images and 4K video as well as 360° spatial audio recording. A spherical image was taken immediately in one shot and was then edited and shared with us in a minute. The camera enables us to create our own virtual tours both for the VR headsets and for our VR room. It allows us to share our creations with parents. If we create a virtual tour of a supermarket for instance, to support students who find going into supermarkets difficult then parents can also take their child through the tour at home on a tablet or iPad. The THETA can be remotely connected to a smartphone. I have written relevant documents for the use of VR headsets in a special school and the documents can be found in the health and safety section of this book.

There are other similar kits now on the market such as ClassVR and Alchemy VR so that they are becoming more affordable for schools to use. These kits also provide augmented reality (AR) experiences.

VR technology is an effective learning tool in a more interactive way than using a film or a TV programme. Our students enjoy the experience and it is highly motivating. It is incumbent upon teachers to ensure planning is in place so that it is used judiciously. I can recall seeing TVs misused in classes and would not wish to see that happen with VR.

VR technology had been available since the mid-twentieth century but it is only now relatively affordable for schools. Traditional forms of teaching do not suit students with learning disabilities. Our students with learning disabilities have made progress

My top six websites where you can access the VR experience are:

1. **Boulevard** is a site that gives VR museum and Art gallery experiences. Boulevard work in parallel with Apple, Google, Samsung, Microsoft, Oculus, and others. HMDs, HoloLens and ARKit-ready iOS devices will give students fully immersive experiences. This is available at: http://blvrd.com/experiences/

2. **Nearpod** is a site that you can purchase VR lessons from. This is available at: https://nearpod.com/s/vr-explorations-F985

3. **YouTube** has its own VR platform at: www.youtube.com/360.

4. **Discovery VR** is available through a mobile app that you can download and watch by moving your iPad or phone to reveal 360-degree views. It can also be a fully immersive experience using a mobile headset like Gear VR or a tethered headset like Oculus Rift. This is available at: https://itunes.apple.com/us/app/discovery-vr/id1030815031?ls=1&mt=8 Other similar apps are available from iTunes such as Aquarium VR. Just go to the app store and search for discovery VR.

5. **Immersive VR Education** is a very exciting site for schools allowing teachers and management to create immersive experiences for free for staff and students. This is available at: http://immersivevreducation.com/

6. **Unimersiv** is an immersive learning platform that teachers can sign up to take students on VR experiences. This is available at: https://unimersiv.com/virtual-reality-schools/?rel=home-top

through the use of VR mainly because it can turn a passive learning experience into an active one.

Virtual classrooms

There are many countries all over the world that are now benefitting from virtual classrooms. In Australia the School of the Air links teachers in town with children in their homes wherever they are. Alice springs has the world's largest classroom running since 1951 with 120 students spread over 1 million square kilometres of central Australia (ASSOA 2018).

In the past in Australia, teachers would post work out by mail and students would post answers back.

It could take weeks for them to find out what they'd done right and what could be improved. In the early 2000s, Australia transitioned to computer- and video-based teaching. Today, families in Australia can enrol their offspring in virtual schools. This is sometimes referred to as cloud-based learning, e-learning or online learning.

In a virtual school often students can only see the teacher unless the teacher clicks on a particular student's video stream. Students can only see each other when teacher clicks on their link and broadcasts it via the teacher feed.

Other virtual schools use web conferencing software which allow you to see your classmates as you log in. It allows for synchronous online provision. On everyone's screen is a chat icon that allows a constant stream of comments, questions and replies. The remainder of the screen is occupied by lesson content. Students in virtual classes would have the same access, depending on the school funds, to VR methods of learning as other ordinary classes.

Teachers stay engaged with the students through a variety of interactive learning aids. In some virtual schools, breakout rooms are used for groups of students to work together on a project before delivering it to the whole class at a later date. There is a lessening of behaviour-related problems in virtual classrooms. Dropbox, Google Drive and Microsoft SkyDrive, among others, can make vital documents available to students and teachers in seconds. Assignments can be emailed or posted up to Internet clouds allowing students to get instant feedback. Virtual schools exist in many countries across the world. In America for instance, a report published by the University of Colorado's National Education policy centre in 2017 counted over a quarter of a million students in the United States enrolled in 528 full-time virtual schools.

Educational funding is a problem worldwide but it is possible for virtual schools to share a timetable and share a teacher by using the same technology. This is cost effective for the governments concerned and often allows students the freedom to support the family business for part of the day and study when it suits. It also saves families on travel and living costs. Virtual learning won't work for all students as a computer, laptop or tablet is needed as well as access to the internet.

Some virtual classes organise actual meetings in the real world a couple of times a year so that students who work together virtually get the opportunity to enhance the virtual learning experience. Advancements in artificial intelligence have led to an explosion in online learning.

Always popular in remote parts of the world there are now free online platforms such as Massive Open Online Courses(MOOCs)[1] and the Massachusetts Institute of Technology (MIT)[2] offers all graduate and undergraduate courses for free online. MIT is pioneering online programmes to support future twenty-first century industries that provide industry-relevant skills and credentials, in a form recognised by leading employers. The Khan Academy allows students from around the world to take free classes in all levels for age two to 100+ online. There is even an offline version known as KA lite.[3]

Notes

1 See item 14 in the Appendix and resources chapter
2 See item 15 in the Appendix and resources chapter
3 See item 16 in the Appendix and resources chapter

Augmented reality (AR) and learning opportunities for children with learning difficulties

Augmentative is a word we are familiar with in special schools when we consider one of the biggest keys to learning – communication. Augmentative and Alternative Communication (AAC) includes simple systems such as pictures, eye movement, gestures, sign language as well as technology. To augment communication means to modify or enhance it.

I have noticed that teachers have always found the use of pictures, PECs cards, signing, use of gestures and eye movement very easy to use with students. I have also noticed that teachers can be hesitant with AAC technology.

Soundbeam[1] is a form of augmented technology. We have a Soundbeam 5 in our school. It enables staff and pupils to create scenes using different sounds from a catalogue of sounds on the machine to enhance reality. Students have used different sounds and music to create a musical performance of *Peter and the Wolf* which they performed nationally, using the sensor based technology in the beams and the switches of Soundbeam 5. Soundbeam 6 now has the ability to add film as a background making it a truly immersive experience. Staff in school have been trained in the use of Soundbeam but only a couple of members of staff choose to use the technology regularly.

There is still a need for teachers to embrace technology and use it as an aid to help communicate the curriculum and as a support for students to visualise their lessons better. The role of the teacher in setting guidelines and creating the context for this new technology is vital.

As technology progresses and traditional teaching methods no longer cut it, teachers have to embrace a different kind of reality in the classroom.

AR caters for visual learners with life-like images so that students can gain understanding on something abstract. They can view the object from different angles to gain perspective. AR supports auditory learners by allowing a student to scan an image that then gives them information to listen to about the image. AR also allows students to hear directions by clicking a button. AR will allow kinaesthetic learners hands-on experiences of a 360° virtual environment that they can move around as if they were actually there. It complements constructivist and collaborative learning.

Warning: When using Augmented Reality please ensure students are aware of their surroundings. It's easy to be completely immersed in the experience and forget where you are!

Augmented reality has been available to schools for a while now using apps. These apps could be considered an introduction to AR.

Apps

Augmented reality apps have been used in our school where the digital object is projected onto the classroom surface (like a hologram). These show up on the school iPad's display using the AR software providing a hands-on practical experience.

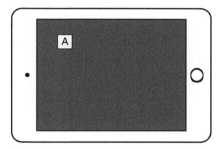

Figure 6.1 Ipad apps

Here are my top 10 free educational apps that can be used on iPads /tablets/Phones/ laptops in the classroom and at home.

Tried and tested AR apps for the classroom

1. **Dinosaurs Everywhere** is a free augmented reality app. Once the teacher has downloaded it for the student and the student activates the camera, dinosaurs can be seen wherever they point the camera. If they touch a dinosaur, the app reveals text information about that dinosaur superimposed over the visuals. Suitable for age 4 and above. (Requires iPhone 4, iPhone 4S, iPod 4th Gen or higher, iPad2, new iPad or higher.) Follow this link: https://itunes. apple.com/gb/app/dinosaurs-everywhere-a-jurassic-experience-in-any-park/ id660029727?mt=8

(Continued)

(*Continued*)

2. If you allow students to take the iPads home as we do then another free app to download onto their iPads if they love space (as one of our students does) is **Star Walk 2 Ads + Sky Guide**. It is suitable for age four and above and is free. It won the Apple Design Award 2010. It is an interactive astrology guide to the night sky. Launch the app and point your iPhone at the night sky, you'll see the stars, planets, satellites, and constellations in their proper place from your location. Tap the AR icon in the upper right corner to add the image from your camera to your sky view. Star Walk even has a Twitter community. Follow this link: https://itunes.apple.com/gb/app/star-walk-2-ads-sky-guide/id1112481571?mt=8

3. The free **Quiver-3D colouring app** is awesome! It combines actual colouring in (you just press print on the app to print out the pages-a Wi-Fi printer is useful) with state of the art augmented reality technology to give students or your own children the wow factor. Every coloured page comes to life and you can play and pause the animation. Some schools have a de-stress station in their class-rooms where paper and crayons, markers sit. Quiver colouring pages can take the station to another level. It's suitable for age four and above. Follow this link: https://itunes.apple.com/gb/app/quiver-3d-coloring-app/id650645305?mt=8

4. **JigSpace** is a free AR app that allows students to view step by step interac-tive 3D breakdowns of complex ideas such as the workings of a toaster. One of my previous students with ASD would have loved it! Suitable for age four plus. Follow this link: https://itunes.apple.com/gb/app/jigspace/id1111193492?mt=8

5. If you have students interested in aircraft then the free AR app named **RAF100 AR Flypast** is worth using. Suitable for age four plus. You actually feel as if you are in the cockpit of an aircraft. The app allows you to collect aircraft and create your own fly past and see it in augmented reality in the school grounds or flying over your own house. Follow this link: https://itunes.apple.com/gb/app/raf100-ar-flypast/id1386126602?mt=8

6. **Catchy Words** is a free AR word game app for age four plus. Immersive experience where you walk around catching the letters with the iPad to solve the word. Family sharing allows six students to play together. Follow this link: https://itunes.apple.com/gb/app/catchy-words/id1266039244?mt=8

7. **Zookazam** is a free AR app that teaches students what animals eat, where they live and their conservation status laced with many other fun and inter-esting facts. Students learn using detailed info-graphics that appear right on the screen with the 3D animal. Explore all the hidden features in ZooKazam by selecting the Settings button. You can add snow or rain to your scene

and even change the educational voice over from teacher to student. Age four plus. Follow this link: https://itunes.apple.com/gb/app/zookazam-free/id1037017116?mt=8

8. **Measurekit** is a fantastic way to get students using measure. Measurekit is a free AR app that allows you to measure different things around you using the iPad (or iPhone) camera using Apple's famous ARKit technology. It contains nine measuring AR tools. Age four plus. Follow this link: https://itunes.apple.com/us/app/ar-measurekit/id1258270451?mt=8

9. **Lego® AR studios.** If you use Lego as a building club therapy in your school as we do, then this free app could be an extension to that. Age four plus. Follow this link: https://itunes.apple.com/gb/app/lego-ar-studio/id1296734986?mt=8

10. **Q Moment AR.** Explore emotions using AR. This app is expensive at £48.99 but it was created specifically to help students with autism learn language skills. It is claimed it can also help those with mental health problems. The app works with a Merge cube which you can buy on Amazon. The merge cube is the world's first holographic educational cube. Age four plus. Follow these links: https://itunes.apple.com/us/app/q-moment-ar/id1262045402?mt=8 or www.amazon.co.uk/MERGE-Cube-Holograms-Winning-Purchase/dp/B0741FNH18

All of the apps above can be used without smartglasses. Smartglasses are set to revolutionise the way we can support students with autism. See Figure 2.5 which shows a pair of smartglasses from 2018.

Emotion Charades[2] is an app for use by students with autism and is available from The Empower Me™ system by Brain Power but is run on Google Glass, an expensive brand of smartglasses. As with any augmented reality, you can still see the world around you. Smartglasses allow the wearer to be hands free and engaged with the social world. With this app, the autistic person sees an emoji floating on either side of the partner's face, and tilts her/his head to choose the one that matches the facial expression, for a reward. Meanwhile, the software automatically monitors her/his performance as well as anxiety or stress level.

All of our students' iPads are individualised to meet the needs of each student so that the technology downloaded is appropriate. Teachers can combine AR learning apps to develop student collaboration and self-learning skills. Technology is capable of transforming the education sector exponentially if all educators embrace it.

Augmented interactive AR textbooks are also in use in classrooms now. More and more publishers are trying to find ways to augment some of their books content. Popar[3] is a company that produces smart books, puzzles and charts to engage children of all ages as they come to life with amazing animations. Our senior and middle management teams are in correspondence with Clever Book[4] to decide whether we should trial an appropriate Augmented Reality books classroom kit. AR books can incorporate audio clips, 3D animations and interactive games into the learning experience.

Outside of the classroom this is the world that the child of today is used to. Children are becoming bored with traditional schooling. Governments around the world have been updating their schools' curriculum to try and secure better outcomes for children. Teachers have a professional responsibility to deliver the curriculum through the best teaching methods possible. Pedagogy should determine our educational use of this new technology and how it might contribute to our set of educational aims. Pedagogy should drive the technology and not the other way around.

Five sites that encourage twenty-first centuryAR skills

1. **Minecraft:** Education Edition is a collaborative and versatile platform that educators can use across subjects to encourage 21st-century skills. It currently has 35 million teachers and students in 115 countries around the world licensed to use the game to transform the way they teach and learn. This is available at: https://education.minecraft.net/class-resources/lessons/

2. **Timelooper** is a site that allows you to step back in time when you visit sites in real time. This is available at: https://www.timelooper.com/

3. **Augthat** is a site that has a very large library of augmented reality based lessons and now cater for special needs too. This is available at: http://augthat.com/index.php/courses/special-needs/

4. **ChromvilleWorld** is a site that encourages children's creativity through technology. It has a science app that helps students understand science much more easily through the use of AR. It also has classroom materials for teachers that are constantly updated. This is available at: https://chromville.com/education/

5. **AR Flashcards** is a site that allows you to print off free flashcards of addition, shape and colour as well as the alphabet and more. You can then download their free app that turns those flashcards into 3D figures that are animated. This is available at: http://arflashcards.com/

If schools had plenty of money, then in the near future we should no longer be seeing desktop computers in classrooms. AR favours ubiquitous computing where computing is made to appear anytime and everywhere in any format. Using smartglasses students will be given super powers and be able to have several computer screens in front of them at one time. They will also be able to have holograms appear at the same time. These smartglasses are available now to those who can afford them but they are currently too expensive for use in the majority of schools.

Ralph Osterhout, recognised by many as a billionaire genius, founded the company ODG in 1999. ODG claim to have the largest extended reality smartglasses portfolio worldwide. In 2012 he made 150 million dollars selling patents to Microsoft and has 200 patents to his name. ODG is one of the companies that supply smartglasses to industries. Its latest development in smartglasses for the consumer are the R-9 glasses. Microsoft have the HoloLens smartglasses. I have seen both demonstrate the huge potential for AR and the way we will view the world.

Many other companies are developing smartglasses for the consumer market. They are a new computing medium that bring people, places and objects from your physical and digital worlds together allowing for communication and shared experiences. Actively engaging learners results in faster learning, better retention, and improved decision making.

It is now possible for augmented reality to lead a lesson. Instead of the teacher or teaching assistant accompanying each individual students and having to remind individual students of what they are looking for the augmented reality glasses informs the student of the facts and may even offer guidance when the student requests it.

A treasure hunt

Treasure hunts are very popular in special schools. I have led treasure hunts in the past where we have sent pupils to communication aids in order to receive another clue. Now with the aid of AR the treasure hunt can be even more exciting.

A map, linked to GPS, can appear in front of their eyes showing them their location and the location of the "treasure" and it can prompt you with a heat map as you get near. The GPS can also inform the actual teacher of where you are. As in any treasure hunt such as Pokeman® it may send you to a person or place on route to receive another clue. Only the person can appear as a hologram instead of being real.

Students with autism, once shown the steps, may even prefer this way of learning. It is dynamic and interactive and there is no invasion of personal space. Engagement is on the student's terms.

Notes

1 See item 17 in the Appendix and resources chapter
2 See item 18 in the Appendix and resources chapter
3 See item 19 in the Appendix and resources chapter
4 See item 20 in the Appendix and resources chapter

7 Artificial intelligence (AR)
Teaching and learning opportunities for students with learning difficulties

Smart learning platforms

These have sprouted up all over the UK. Smart platforms are designed to allow educators to master additional skills and receive continuous and automated feedback, and when used strategically have the potential to help improve performance and increase student progress.

A typical smart platform is Wales' bilingual virtual learning platform named Hwb. Hwb allows its users to design digital curriculum and content across devices and is the Welsh government's programme for improving the use of digital technology in schools. It gives access to a range of free digital tools and resources that can support and assist the transformation of digital classroom practices. Online resources can be accessed anywhere, at any time and from a range of web-enabled devices. It also provides tools to help education practitioners create and share their own resources and assignments. All Hwb users are provided with free access to Microsoft Office 365 which has additional free apps and facilities.

New artificial intelligence systems are being developed to help teachers assess students more effectively (Georgopoulos et al. 2003) that could uncover some of the learning disabilities that are difficult to diagnose. Once they can be properly identified, educators can tap into the resources available for a learning disability.

AI virtual digital assistants

An easy classroom introduction to artificial intelligence (AI) is to set up either Amazon's Alexa, Apple's Siri, Microsoft's Cortana or Google's Assistant in the classroom and start getting it to answer some of the questions that occur during lessons. Students with autism can sometimes find social interaction threatening and so virtual assistants, though still in their infancy, could enable a person with autism to have sustained conversations for hours

54

on end about something that they may be very interested in. A student with a learning difficulty could ask the virtual assistant the same question repeatedly because machines are infinitely more patient than humans. We have several children in our school who would love getting the correct answer to the same question repeated over and over again.

AI virtual assistants don't pass judgement and are not socially threatening. We have found in our school that our students are more interested in learning when it involves technology. AI virtual assistants will probably not fully replace teachers and teaching assistants but could serve as an invaluable extension in the classroom, helping teachers to more effectively meet the personal learning needs and style of students simultaneously.

AI robots

Companies have been developing and creating robots and virtual human robots for use in a variety of educational and therapeutic environments for more than a decade. Games and activities with the robot can be designed to be suitable for the development of communication skills and how to accept and obey social rules at the same time. Children learn to socialise through imitation. We have found that students in our school are less overwhelmed by puppets and robots than they would be by a human.

Robots used for this purpose can be divided into two types: humanoid robots and toy-like robots. Humanoid robots appear similar to humans. They may express a human voice and perform physical actions, i.e. facial expressions, hand gestures and body movement. Below is a selection of robots that have been used with students who have communication difficulties:

Keepon® Pro is a manufactured by BeatBots LLC. It is little yellow puffball robot at 25cm high, developed by Hideki Kozima for autism therapy in 2003. It doesn't speak, can't manipulate objects, and has one facial expression. The robot is placed in the room with the student while the therapist remotely controls it from another room. It was priced at $30,000 in 2009. A toy version was madeavailable on Amazon.com for $163.99 in 2018 and called My Keepon. To find out more go to https://beatbots. net/keepon-pro

SoftBank Robotics manufacture **Nao**®, who was developed in 2004. Nao is a program-mable social autonomous robot. Nao is 58cm in height and weighs 5.6kg. The manufacturers have developed programmes and apps to use for special education though it is available for use in many different disciplines. In 2018, it is in its fifth version and about 10,000 Nao have already been sold throughout the world. The cost of a Nao in 2018 is approximately £6,500.

SoftBank also manufacture **Pepper**®, a taller cousin to Nao. Pepper is 1.2m (4ft) and weighs 28kg (62lb) and is also a programmable autonomous talking humanoid robot.

Pepper can identify joy, sadness, anger or surprise and respond appropriately. It has a 10.1in touchscreen which allows the integration of web pages, applications and images. I met Pepper at a recent AI conference.[1] In 2018 Pepper cost £14,300. To find out more go to www.softbankrobotics.com/emea/en/robots/buying-a-robot

iCat®, "interactive Cat", was developed by the Dutch Philips Research team in 2005. The robot has a bright yellow body and white face. It is meant to resemble a cat and is approximately 40cm high. iCat® was developed as an open interactive robot platform with emotional feedback to investigate social interaction. It can look happy, surprised, angry and sad. It can understand voice commands as well as recognise faces and gestures. It can select music or movies, make appointments or read the weather to you. For the time being Philips only sell these to universities and research labs. To find out more go to www.roboticstoday.com/robots/icat

The University of Hertfordshire's Adaptive Systems Research Group began testing **Kaspar**®, a humanoid robot, to develop and practice social skills in 2007. They conduct pioneering research into artificial intelligence and robotics. Kaspar is a child-sized humanoid robot. designed as a social companion to improve the lives of children with autism and other communication difficulties. The research team are currently looking for funding for five pre-production Kaspar robots that can be trialled in UK primary schools before they can be made available for purchase. For more information contact www.herts.ac.uk/kaspar/contacts-and-useful-links

Robots 4 autism and Hanson Robotics® in America began developing **Milo**® in 2011. Milo is a humanoid robot to develop and practice social skills. They claim that students with autism can improve and they shared with me the fact that a student had "improved three grades in a 9-month period and that her growth, both academically and socially, has been remarkable". Milo is just under two feet in height, weights 4.5kg, and has the face of a young boy. He has a camera in his right eye and visual algorithms to detect colours, motion, faces and QR codes. He has the ability to identify and respond to emotions. The cost for a Milo robot including the curriculum programme in 2018 is $5,000. To find out more contact greg@robokind.com

Romibo® is a social therapy robot created by Aubrey Shick and Garth Zeglin. Romibo entered classrooms in 2013 and is sold by Origami Robotics, based in America. Romibo moves on two wheels and is 28cm tall. It weighs 3kg and is furry with a choice of colour. It has two eyes on a computerised screen that can follow faces and hold a person's gaze and it can talk. The iPad that controls its movement also allows Romibo to say words and phrases typed into the iPad. In 2018 Romibo cost $698.

Aubrey Schick has also designed **VibeAttire** which is a tactile-audio wearable computer designed to allow hearing-impaired users to experience rich sound. For more information go to http://socialtech.strikingly.com/

Vibroacoustic therapy

Our school uses two artificial intelligence-based electric machines known as a vibroacoustic (VA) beds. One is portable and has the music already programmed on it.

It is a Vibroacoustic Therapy System with music inbuilt and is available from Relax-UK.com.

The other one is linked up to a water bed that is embedded with speakers. Training for the use of vibroacoustic therapy can be provided by Soundbeam trainers. The following link takes you to our YouTube site and a video of the therapy being given: https://youtu.be/Ocp1buvwSS8?list=PL-a5MUplgI4nVMUEFGUGFg4jTxjvPyLur

The speakers emit highly specific frequency programs that are mastered for VA therapy.

Vibroacoustic therapy focuses on the haptic sensations to give the students and adults with learning disabilities who have experienced it a sense of wellbeing. It has also been used with a mainstream student with terminal cancer. His mother reported that it helped him to remain calm. VA therapy uses sound to produce vibrations that are felt directly by the body.

During the four years that we have provided this therapy we have seen success with both children and adults. There are a variety of impacts seen as a direct result of vibroacoustic therapy in the area of communication. The therapy has significantly boosted confidence enabling students to converse with the therapist in different surroundings, and built on relationships with peers.

A colleagues of mine, the therapist, Julie Fallows, has noted that:

* Student's bodies visibly release tension during sessions.
* Their joints, muscles show ease of movement, uncurling of fists/fingers. This has been proved when replacing clothing, splints, shoes after a session.
* Further reports have been received from adult carers that their clients become motivated for the day, helps with sleep patterns.
* General wellbeing lifted.
* Medically it has helped children and adults with bowel problems as the low frequency tones reach organs creating internal massage.

Neurofeedback – brain training

Neurofeeback is an artificial intelligence-based electric machine that provides brain training. Neurofeedback training is the only scientifically proven method to train the brain. Neurofeedback has research backing supporting its non-invasive

Figure 7.1 Neurofeedback Training

effectiveness and use in depression, attention deficit disorder, anxiety, sleep disorders, headaches and migraines, and other emotional issues (Orndorff-Plunkett et al. 2017). It can also be used to help those with autism and cerebral palsy. Some neurofeedback devices have algorithms for synthetic outputs such as attention, meditation, emotional range, etc.

Our school delivers neurofeedback to some of our students. There are different neurofeedback systems available that are used in hospitals, schools and therapy centres around the world. We use the NeurOptimal® brain training system from a company based in the USA. We have had some success with it. Neurofeedback is pretty straightforward to deliver. Once someone has been trained in its delivery they in turn can train other staff. Once the machine is set up the student can play a game or watch a film.

A student with attention deficiency hyperactive disorder (ADHD) and emotional behavioural difficulties (EBD) received neurofeedback training with very good results.[2] We received weekly reports from home that the student was now sleeping through the night. Something the student had not experienced before. We were also informed that at home he was able to reason things out. The same positive feedback came from the classroom teacher.

A team of neuroscientists from the Universities of Cambridge, Japan and the USA are combining neurofeedback with artificial intelligence to remove a fear memory from the brain. The technique is called "Decoded Neurofeedback" and uses algorithms (Koizumi et al 2016).

Eye Gaze

Eye Gaze systems are artificial intelligence-based electric devices. Our school uses the Tobii® eye tracker system. Algorithms are the intelligence of the eye tracker that are processed either on the computer or on a dedicated processor. The algorithms control the sensors and the illuminators. Based on the sensor images they identify and calculate the position of the eyes, where the user is looking and the size of the students. Developed over 15 years Tobii EyeCore® is the leading eye tracking algorithm. It is the world's most powerful eye-tracking algorithm core.

Tobii® claim that it is extremely robust and that it will work on virtually all people under all specified conditions. Their team have been particularly helpful in setting it up in our school and returning regularly to provide training to staff.

We have a teaching assistant who sets it up daily and has a daily timetable of students receiving the support. Other staff are also trained to use the device and will also use it with students.

It is potentially life-changing for students with severe physical disabilities who are unable to control a computer through a mouse or keyboard or are unable to use other communication aids which work through touch, for example, via a switch or touch-screen. Cameras pick up light reflection from the student's eye as the student scans a screen. Movements of the student's eye are translated into movements of a cursor through infrared technology using a camera to detect the reflection of near infra-red light on the cornea and student of each eye in order to determine where the eye gaze is directed.

We are in our second year of using Eye Gaze technology at our school. An Eye Gaze computer is available and used daily with those students who benefit from this approach. Prior to this, we use a Perspex Etran frame choice board to build up skills such as tracking between objects, fixing gaze and making a choice. As the students acquire these skills they transfer to using the Eye Gaze computer.

Eye Gaze technology allows us to observe what our students see, attend to and track on screen; what they notice and don't notice, what they prefer to look at and what sense they make of what they see. Such understanding of our most complex students are already making us change our teaching practice with these students. The analysis tools are really useful for showing progress.

Students are using the technology to achieve educational goals. Our B Squared assessment tool is showing that some students have made terrific progress since using Eye Gaze. Three of our students have made the big jump from a P level 3 across all subjects where they are classed as having profound and multiple learning difficulties (PMLD) to a P level 4 across all subjects. P level 1 to P level 3 describes early learning and development before students begin to engage in subject-specific learning; P level 4 representing the entry point to subject-specific learning. Some students who may still be

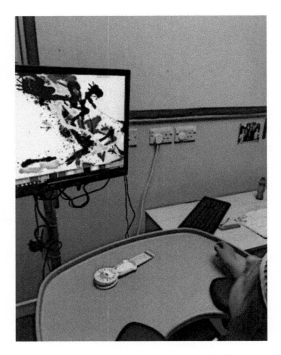

Figure 7.2 Eye Gaze – cause and effect

at P level 3 and below in most areas of the curriculum are performing well in computer skills.

Figure 7.2 is a picture of one of our students who is at the early stages of Eye Gaze using cause and effect. When the student looks at the screen they can create a picture using the colour palette at the bottom of the screen.

Eye Gaze is also opening up wider opportunities for our students to interact and engage. One of our students, with cerebral palsy, confined to a wheelchair and with learning difficulties, has been using the Tobii Eye Gaze machine for six months. Other access methods tried from Nursery through to Key Stage 2 had little to no success.

As you can see from Figure 7.3, the student is now able to access a field of 22 icons and speaks in two to four word phrases.

Eye Gaze devices have the capacity to give students the ability to use standard applications such as Word, to surf the Internet, communicate by email, play online games, use Facebook or Skype. As technology continues to progress the possibilities for developing Eye Gaze technology are endless. Interest in and a desire to own and use high-tech Eye Gaze systems is escalating with our parents who wish to continue offering it at home. Though the cost has come down in recent years, I would advise chasing a grant or charity to assist in the purchase. The Steve Morgan Foundation has funded Eye Gaze devices for parents of students at our school.

Figure 7.3 Eye Gaze possibilities

Guide to using Eye Gaze

1. Turn on the electricity at the wall.

2. At the back of the monitor there is a black box – press the circle button that is on the back of the box once.

3. Once the screen is loaded find the Eye Gaze folder to the right of the screen and open it.

4. On the right side on the toolbar there is a box with a list of the pupils' names on it who attend. Click it and scroll until you find the pupil required,

5. Once you have found the correct pupil's name, click on it.

6. Once the pupil's screen pops up, you will need to go to the bottom right of the screen and click APPLY,

7. It will then let you make sure the pupil is seated in a good position – as long as you can get the two white dots in between the yellowish green area they will be fine. Some pupils only seem to pick up one eye – that's ok as long as it is in the right area. However, some pupils who use it are not easy to get positioned and comfortable in a wheelchair – extra support maybe needed,

(Continued)

(*Continued*)

8. Then go to the bottom of the screen again and click OK.

9. You can then start the Eye Gaze session.

10. Back on the main screen there are four folders: Eye FX, Communicator, and two more.

11. Eye FX is mainly for starting pupils off on different games for them to try, or for tracking, targeting etc.

12. Communicator is an app that also has a lot of things like matching, jigsaws, exploring, turn taking etc. It can also be used with students to enable them to ask for things.

13. To get on to Communicator you have to click the folder then wait for it to load (sometimes this takes a while). On the first page double click on page set up, and wait for it to load. There are a few RG apps in the saved folder to the right of the screen. There are also colour match games in there.

14. The other two apps are for tracking and turn taking.

15. Once the session has finished you need to repeat from step 3.

16. At end of the session go to the bottom left of screen and press shut down. Then turn off the electricity at the wall.

Technological advances

Phones and tablets today are able to translate text to voice for our students. There are hundreds of apps available for use on these devices, often for free, that make life easier for students with a host of different learning issues. Just a few of these, that I have seen in action, are listed below:

Seeing AI This is a Microsoft Research project. It is free app that narrates the surrounding world for the visually disabled. Using artificial intelligence for image recognition and natural language processing it can describe nearby people and their emotions. It delivers on product recognition reading bar codes, speaks text both typed and handwritten and has document functions. One of our students who has moved on to a secondary school benefits from its use. Other companies are bringing out similar apps.

Helpicto Equadex developed the Helpicto app with Microsoft Cognitive Services REST APIs and Microsoft Azure tools. The Helpicto app is free and available on several app sites. The Helpicto app uses artificial intelligence to alleviate communication difficulty and it provides a visual representation of language. This is suitable for use with anyone who has language difficulties or is nonverbal.

What does it actually do? Imagine that a teacher may be trying to communicate with a nonverbal student with ASD, for example. That student may not be able to process what is being said and could get anxious. Instead of causing distress the teacher can use their iPad to speak their request to Helpicto.

Helpicto parses the meaning of the request and presents a series of pictograms that show the student what the teacher wanted to communicate. With one look at the screen the student can move on to follow the visual cues. The company currently offers the app on the French market but intends to release it globally in the near future. Be aware it is currently available in French only and you may be required to pay for add-ons (as happens with many apps today). Follow this link: https://itunes.apple.com/go/app/helpicto/id1345333575

If you want to follow Helpicto on Twitter, so that you know when the English version becomes available, then follow this link: https://Twitter.com/Helpicto

WaytoB This is a new app for use on a smartwatch was created by Trinity College Dublin. It will allow students with learning difficulties to go back and for to school or college and even to new places independently. There are two parts to the app – one part for the user and the other part for the friend or relative to customise to make sure the user is always safe. It provides the following important features: turn-by-turn directions (arrows and audio) based on the user's orientation and prompted by vibration or audio cue; walking instructions integrated with public transport, live tracking of the user's location; accessible panic button to easily initiate contact between connected pair. It is currently being trialled in Ireland. To find out more go to: https://waytob.com/

AI Chatbots There are many AI chatbot apps. These allow students to chat with the bot and improve their conversational language. It allows them to practice casual day-to-day interactions; practice asking and answering questions and chatting about topics that interest them. English with Andy – Chat & Learn is available for free by following this link: https://itunes.apple.com/gb/app/english-with-andy-chat-learn/id1078490509?mt=8

Recent News Recent News is a smart news app which provides students with a latest news with artificial intelligence option. They can easily watch news that are of a particular interest. Students with autism love this aspect of it. There are thousands of different topics in this app that can be chosen from and it remembers the student's preferences unless it is decided they need changing. Follow the link to their site and choose how you wish to download: http://www.recent.io/

DataBot DataBot is a virtual audible assistant that can talk with you. It is another good artificial intelligence app which can also be use as virtual talking robot. Teachers or parents could show students how to set it up. You can name it and also choose a name for yourself. It takes some practice to ensure you use the right kind of words that DataBot recognises. Once you do, it has many different options to explore and use.

Notes

1   See item 21 in the Appendix and resources chapter
2   See item 22 in the Appendix and resources chapter

8 Health and safety implications in the technological age

Klaus Schwab describes this era we are living in as the fourth industrial revolution which, according to the world economic forum (WEF), will be a "fusion of technologies that is blurring the lines between the physical, digital and biological spheres". We will face new and different health and safety risks. For example, prolonged use of VR (using headsets) should be avoided, as this could negatively impact eye-hand coordination, balance and multi-tasking ability. This chapter will go through some of the health and safety risks associated with this technological age.

Online safety

Parents of today's children have little if any experience of the online world that their children navigate so easily. The online world crept into our lives so stealthily that many parents are ignorant of its power and attraction. Several young autistic men in the UK have been, and still are being prosecuted for hacking into military computer networks and suchlike (Dunn 2017). They tend not to think of the consequences when they are trawling networks and their parents have no idea that they are causing havoc until police officers knock on the front door.

The internet is a form of communication. It reaches more people globally than any other communication channel. Every second four new members joins a social media site to communicate instantly and for free. Children are able to keep in constant touch with friends who are also online. Facebook now have a page for *Children using social media* where they can share live commentaries on what they are doing and where they are going. Potentially anyone online can read that information. In America Enough is Enough (EIE) was formed in 1992 to make the internet safer for children and families. Internet Safety 101 was created by EIE in partnership with the US Department of Justice in 2008 to deliver critical Internet safety resources to parents and educators.

In Australia the office of the eSafety Commissioner leads online safety education for the Australian government providing resources and support materials for parents, carers and educators throughout Australia.

In 1998, the British Educational Communications and Technology Agency (BECTA) began providing advice and guidance to British schools and local authorities on all aspects of e-safety, in conjunction with the Department for Education and skills (DfES). In 2015 a new agreement with ICT services for Education, replaced the BECTA agreement. South West Grid for Learning (SWGfL) are now the coordinators of the UK Safer Internet Centre. They provide resources and training for schools in the UK designed specifically for education. They also provide support material for parents. They offer everyone who works with children and young people the European Pedagogical ICT (EPICT) Online Safety Qualification.

Our school is in Wales and the Welsh government provide schools with the Hwb learning platform. The Welsh Government has contracted with South West Grid for Learning (SWGfL) to promote the safe and responsible use of Hwb and provide a range of online safety activities across Wales. These activities include online safety training for education professionals and school governors, and developing resources to support children, parents and teachers.

In February 2017, the Online Safety Zone was launched on Hwb to provide guidance and information for schools about online safety. Parents and students can also access the zone. It has a range of useful resources and links to training in online safety. It also includes access to the 360° safe Cymru tool, an award winning online safety self-assessment tool for schools.

Safer Internet Day is an awareness-raising campaign that started in Europe fourteen years ago, and is now celebrated in more than 100 countries. It's coordinated by the Brussels-based Insafe Network for the European Commission.

In Great Britain, by law, each Local Authority must have a Local Safeguarding Children Board (LSCB). These boards are joint agency groups that are responsible for child welfare in their area. The LSCBs write policy guidelines for safeguarding children, ensure that the different agencies work together and conduct inquiries into serious cases or child deaths. It is within their remit to review the Online Safety provision across the agencies and organisations that work with children in their area and to develop an area wide strategic plan for Online Safety.

A major challenge for schools in the twenty-first century is to prepare a generation of children to become critical and safe users of information and communication technologies. Schools have to put policies and procedures in place to ensure safe use of communications technologies by the children and young people in their care. Local authorities will often provide guidance for schools on this. Becta Schools website still exists and offers advice and guidance to school leadership teams on how technology can be built into teaching, learning and management. All statutory guidance and legislation published on their site continues to reflect the current legal position unless indicated otherwise.

Teachers themselves need to be educated about the opportunities and risks posed by new technologies. Their e-safety and digital competence development needs to be part of a continuous professional development process and this should commence during induction of new staff. Hwb supports this training. As a school we also use EduCare for Education to provide this training to staff, which is conveniently done via e-learning. The service combines a broad range of online courses with a robust reporting suite that can evidence learning to inspectors.

CEOP offer the interactive 'Thinkuknow' programme and training for teachers. This provides knowledge of online issues, necessary child protection information and training on how to deliver the CEOP presentation. This training can be found at: www.thinkuknow.co.uk/teachers

It is possible for teachers to gain a University Certificate in Child Safety on the Internet. This provides training for teachers to enable them to promote safe and responsible use of internet and mobile technologies and services. The certificate is validated by UCLAN and information can be found at: www.internetsafetyzone.co.uk

A child or young person with learning difficulties may be particularly vulnerable to e-safety risks. In addition to the documents and policies that a special school provides[1] teachers will need to provide additional advice on safe behaviours and what they should never disclose to others online.

Online education platform Whoo's Reading provides free resources for teachers and includes a 10-point list of 'working online rules' from Jessica Sanders (2005).

These rules include:

- Only visit pre-approved internet sites – if you want a site approved ask the teacher.
- Never give out personal information online – people asking for information online are strangers.
- Tell the teacher if you see something uncomfortable or inappropriate- the teacher can report it.
- Ask for teacher's permission before downloading or printing anything.
- Do not change settings without permission.
- Leave the technology space tidy for others to use.
- Do not eat or drink around technology devices – you could break the thing you enjoy using.
- Be gentle with mouse and keyboard – if they break you will not be able to use them.
- Charge devices that are not currently being used – you may want to use them later.

In our school we would have to regularly go through these points with students who go online. Our students are aged two to 11. We find that we have to restrict access to some sites or even block a site that may be inappropriate for that student.

It could also be useful to get consent from parents for their child to go online in school whilst sharing the school rules with them, and asking them if they wish to contribute to the rules. We tend to send information booklets home to parents. We ask parents about their child's technology habits at home and what their rules are. Do they give time limits for the use of game stations or internet use? It can foster a sense of collaboration with parents so that you're not doing anything in class that could contradict with what they're doing at home.

As a school we have rules for responsible use. These rules are intended keep our students safe and help them to be fair to others and they are discussed with those students who are able to understand.

For the majority of our students, who are aged four to 11, we use Communicate in Print for a computer schedule as most of our students find it difficult to process

Student rules for responsible use of a computer

- I will only access the system with my own identity and password, which I will keep secret.
- I will not access other people's files.
- I will only use the computers for school work and homework.
- I will not bring in any removable media, such as memory stick or CD, from outside school unless I have been given permission.
- I will ask permission from a member of staff before using the Internet.
- I will only email people I know or my teacher has approved.
- The messages I send will be polite and responsible.
- A file will only be sent with my email message if it has been checked and is free from viruses and if my teacher has approved sending the file.
- I will not give my home address or telephone number or arrange to meet someone.
- I will not disclose any other person's name, address or any of their personal details.
- I will report any unpleasant material or messages sent to me. I understand this report would be confidential and would help protect other students and myself.
- I understand that the school may check my computer files, including electronic mail messages, and may monitor the Internet sites I visit.

information once they are in an excited state as they often are when using the computer or iPad. Because of copyright issues I reproduce it below using Picto-Selector, a free, comprehensive and convenient picture creator for schedules etc.

You can download this free for yourself if you go to www.pictoselector.eu/home-2/download/ Please be aware that as it is free there is a lot of advertising on the site with big green buttons and the word Download. These are not Picto-Selector and they are not free. The Picto-Selector download is easy to miss among the adverts. It is an amazing free tool and you can make a donation to the site if you are going to make use of the tool regularly.

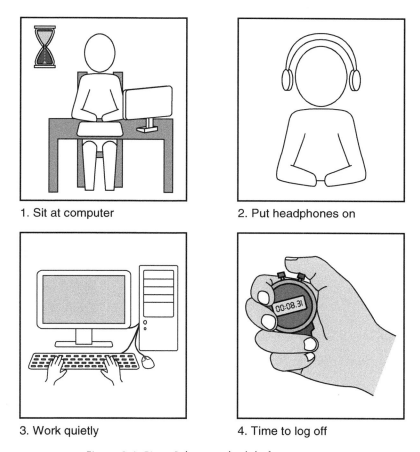

1. Sit at computer

2. Put headphones on

3. Work quietly

4. Time to log off

Figure 8.1 Picto-Selector schedule for computer use

Computer schedule

In addition, we have an acceptable user's policy that we adapted from Flintshire county council's model policy available on their website and our own e-safety policy.[2]

Cyber

Our students today have been completely normalized by digital technologies—it is a fully integrated aspect of their lives (Green and Hannon 2007, p. 21). However, they need to be informed students.

- **Cybersafety** Involves conduct or behavioural concerns of students using their smart-phones for such things as cyber bullying and happy slapping filming fights and ridiculing teachers.
- **Cybercrime** Involves illegal activity. An example would be online fraud.
- **Cybersecurity** Involves unauthorised access or attacks on a computer system. For example, hacking into someone's social media service account or sending a virus to someone's computer via an email.

I was observing in a class on Friday this week and a group of 10-year-olds with autism were telling me of their future ambitions. The only girl amongst suddenly piped up with "I play a game online and I make sure that I never give my email address to anyone in case I get spammed and the computer gets hacked."

Where did that come from? It was nothing to do with what was being discussed but she was informing us of what she wanted us to teach her about. As a Pioneer school for the Welsh Government we have been working on piloting the new curriculum for Wales. The new curriculum for Wales intends giving students more of a say in what they are taught. We need to ensure that we listen to our students and deliver an appropriate education.

Strategies that need to be put in place in schools are:

- Risk assessments related to online use.
- All schools should have an Acceptable user policy.
- Curriculum content referring to safe and responsible use of digital technology.
- School council representative for the management of digital technology at the school.
- Vigilance of the whole school community in preventing and responding to incidents.

Parent responsibilities

Internet safety, it would appear, is a shared responsibility between the internet industry and the public but parents are the first line of defence when protecting their children against internet dangers. Yet they are often overwhelmed when it comes to internet safety issues.

Parents usually know their children's friends and their families. They decide if they will allow them to play at their friends' home. In their own homes parents sometimes have a false sense of security when their child is in in another room perhaps, accessing an internet game that "all my friends are playing". I recall a parent coming to see me a number of years ago to tell me that she went into her nine-year-old daughter's bedroom at 10pm to find her still awake, wearing a microphone headset chatting and playing an Xbox game online with a group of adult males. Her daughter, who was diagnosed with severe emotional and behavioural difficulties (SEBD), was furious with her mother for interrupting the game. In order to support children online parents must first understand their children's online behaviours in order to recognise the risks. It is good practice for schools to offer this kind of awareness training to parents.

Parents of young children need to be aware that before they download a new app, buy a connected toy or create an account on a new platform for their child that they could use a search engine to locate reviews and they could use PEGI (Pan European Game Information) or ESBR (Entertainment Software Rating Board) to check the ratings for age appropriateness, content, levels of violence and profane language. Online safety support is available to us all and it is up to us to choose to use the support available.

Here are some current useful e-safety resources available for parents:

www.childnet.com/kia/parents has educational resources to support teachers, parents and children.

http://swgfl.org.uk/ provides some useful e-safety resources.

http://thinkuknow.co.uk/ tackles online grooming, and provides information about how to protect your child.

www.saferinternet.org.uk provides e-safety tips, advice and resources to help children and young people stay safe on the internet.

Use **http://ceop.police.uk** to report abuse or grooming to Child Exploitation and Online Protection.

The NSPCC provides on-line safety information for parents on their new **E-Safety Link**.

Hector the E-Safety Dolphin is a child-friendly safety button, available for download at home in both Windows and Mac OS formats.

Pan European Game Information provides information for parents and carers on age ratings.

The four big internet providers in the UK – BT, Sky, TalkTalk and Virgin Media – provide their customers with free **Internet Parental Controls** which can be activated at any time. Video guides to help you to download and set-up the controls offered by your provider are available on the UK Safer Internet Centre website.

Virtual reality

Virtual reality (VR) replaces the real world with a simulated one. We have already had issues with our special school students with learning difficulties who sometimes find it difficult leaving the Play Station world. For many young people the virtual world is very much their reality.

It is on public record that Jon Venables, child murderer, had supposedly watched a violent murder video then copied aspects of the video during the murder of James Bulger. Both of his siblings had learning difficulties and attended special needs schools. Jon himself was thought to have learning difficulties.

It is quite easy to ensure students have limited exposure to virtual and augmented reality whilst in school. It is also worth noting that it would be highly irregular for students to be shown inappropriate material during lesson time in school. It makes sense though for there to be guidelines drawn up on how to use this technology sensibly and for the guidelines to be shared with parents.

Here are some things to communicate to the parents first:

- How the technology will be used in school.
- Types of technology that will be used.
- Rules students will be expected to follow.
- Safety precautions you'll be taking and forms for the parents to complete.
- Share the guidance used in school with parents as VR is becoming a very popular form of entertainment and students may want to use it at home.

Figure 8.2 Informing Parents

Virtual reality headset health and safety usage guidance for special schools

Before using the headset:

* Parent consent forms to be completed.
* Medical screening form to be completed.
* A risk assessment form to be completed for each group of pupils using headsets.
* Teachers must not allow the headset to knowingly be used by a pupil with an infectious condition.
* The headset must be cleaned between each use.
* Teacher to make sure the headset is level and secured comfortably on pupil's head.
* Teacher demonstrate how to adjust the viewing focus for each user before use of the headset.
* Teacher to set volume levels so that pupils are not exposed to high volume levels which could damage their hearing.
* Do not use the product if any part is broken, damaged or any wires are exposed.
* Virtual reality headsets cannot be used without adult supervision.

Using the headset

* Teacher to read out all instructions provided with the headset.
* Pupils to follow instructions provided by teacher.
* Teacher to limit sessions to five minutes to start with so that pupils grow accustomed to this form of virtual reality and increase the time gradually to 30 minutes maximum.
* Teacher to investigate any pupil feeling nausea or any discomfort and if necessary halt its use.
* Teacher to monitor use as prolonged use could affect hand-eye coordination and balance.
* Teacher to remain vigilant as this is an immersive experience and pupils will not be aware of their surroundings and could trip or fall while engrossed in the experience.

After using the headset

* Use of the headset may cause loss of balance immediately after using the headset.
* It is not advisable to follow a VR headset session with a PE session.
* Prolonged use of the headsets can lead to tiredness and blurred vision.
* Teacher to rate Google Expedition content in view of any follow up symptoms.

Special school VR headset screening form

Table 8.1 VR headset screening form

Name of student	
Date of birth	
Address	
Telephone number	
Name and telephone number of emergency contact	
Primary diagnosis	
Any other relevant factors	
Weight	
Height	

Important: If you answer **YES** to any of the questions, please consult your GP to ask if they have any objection to your child using Virtual Reality Headsets and sign in the appropriate space below. Please answer with as much detail as possible.

Table 8.2 VR consent form

Condition	Yes	No
Circulatory disorders (high/low blood pressure, Phlebitis, Heart condition, Thrombosis etc.		
Psychotic Conditions		
Allergies		
Diabetes		
Epilepsy		
Headaches/Migraines		
Cancer/Multiple Sclerosis		
Skin disorder or infection		
Active or acute inflammation		
Binocular vision abnormality		
Impaired balance		
Haemorrhaging or Active Bleeding		
Hypertension		
Arthritis		
Recent accident, head, neck injuries, fractures, sprains or injuries		
Prolapsed invertebral disc		
Medication		
Any operations less than 6 months ago		

If you have answered YES to any of the questions above, please sign below to say you have obtained your GP's oral non-objection.

Signed: Date:

By signing this declaration, you agree to follow any protocols put in place to ensure the safety of students at our school.

Table 8.3 VR headset risk assessment

Directorate		Activity (Brief Description)	Virtual Reality Headset	
Service	Education	People at Risk	Pupils and staff	
Location	Special school	Date		Review Date
Assessor		Issue Number	1	

Item No	Hazard (Include Defects)	RISK RATING (without controls) High/Medium/Low	Existing Control Measures	RISK RATING (with existing controls) High/Medium/Low
	1. Sickness/ nausea	med	• General discomfort • Headache • Sweating • Fatigue, • Drowsiness • Disorientation	Low

Seizures	High	• Watch out for involuntary muscle twitches and loss of balance as a potential problem • Have Pupil s Care Plan • Medication i.e buccal to be with pupil • Member of staff trained, knowledgeable and understanding medical condition of the pupil using virtual reality headset • Repeat in seizures during session. Stop use of headset	
Time		Time limit needs to be set for each session	Low
Eye strain		Look for symptoms such as rubbing of the eyes, squinting.	Low
Sickness and general illness		Virtual reality headset could make the pupil feel worse	Low

FURTHER ACTION REQUIRED TO REDUCE RISKS TO ACCEPTABLE LEVEL

Ultimate Risk	HIGH	Ultimate Existing Risk	LOW
Item No	Further Action necessary to control risk	Action By	Date Completed	RESIDUAL RISK (with further controls) High/Medium/Low
Assessor(s) Signature(s)	Managers Name		Manager Signature	
Other relevant Risk Assessments:				

Artificial intelligence

The risks here are more to do with the AI making errors because the data the AI has been given is incorrect. In schools this could mean that the assessments of students are wrong. AI learns to detect patterns and act according to their input.

AI is able to use a basic form of algorithmic optimization to capture attention and make games addictive. These games can be played on the usual games console, an iPad or even a smartphone. There may need to be rules and time limits regarding online games both in school and at home. Some schools may decide that online games or downloaded games even are not suitable for school whilst other schools run their whole curriculum around the use of computer games.[3]

Artificial intelligence provides masses of information on smartphones today. Some schools allow the use of smartphones because of their usefulness. In our VR headsets we have phones that enable the students to have an amazing experience. They do not have messaging or calling capabilities.

We have a school mobile phones policy[4] as I imagine most schools do and in Great Britain it is up to the individual school whether students are allowed to use theirs in school.

Smartphones can be used to access the internet and teachers in our school have found that particularly useful with their own phones when the school system is not working. Smartphones are also used by our parents to send payments into school and they can receive scanned photos of their child's accomplishments straight to their phone.

For older students the smartphone can be used to take a photo of scheduled home-work, and send assignments via e-mails to teachers. QR codes can be scanned which are linked to project related websites. Some apps like SIMS Student have been designed to help students so they can see how they are progressing against targets and receive reminder alerts. At home they may use their own smartphone to access to the internet for research and to answer emails. School could be the right place to educate them about email scams. Collaboration online between students on school-based projects is an important skill to teach students. When a mobile phone is used for educational purposes then students can be more engaged, informed and motivated and can start to use a phone responsibly.

As more and more students are given smartphones by parents to enable them to keep in touch it becomes important to teach students how to use a smartphone safely in the same way that we educate them on the use of an iPad or a computer. It is particularly important for a student with learning difficulties to be educated in how to set up a phone with a sim card and how to use a phone correctly. Students also need to beshown how to use phone apps such as WaytoB, the app that supports students with learning difficulties to travel on their own (a link can be found in Chapter 7).

Schools need to find ways to work mobile phones into the curriculum and help students to

be responsible users of technology. It is vitally important that schools start accepting these tools as tools in order to educate students in correct usage. The same could be said for any twenty-first century technology that enters the classroom whether it is the latest bionic prosthetic limb or the latest pair of smartglasses. If teachers teach respectful and appropriate use of technology in the classroom and use it to build skills as well, then students will feel that the education they are receiving is meaningful and having a real impact on their lives. ·

Notes

1 See item 23 in the Appendix and resources chapter
2 See item 23 in the Appendix and resources chapter
3 See item 5 in the Appendix and resources chapter
4 See item 23 in the Appendix and resources chapter

Appendix and resources

1 The Land of Counterpane

When I was sick and lay a-bed,
I had two pillows at my head,
And all my toys beside me lay
To keep me happy all the day.

And sometimes for an hour or so
I watched my leaden soldiers go,
With different uniforms and drills,
Among the bed-clothes, through the hills;

And sometimes sent my ships in fleets
All up and down among the sheets;
Or brought my trees and houses out,
And planted cities all about.

I was the giant great and still
That sits upon the pillow-hill,
And sees before him, dale and plain,
The pleasant land of counterpane.

2 Moore's Law

Everyone wants better, cheaper, faster and more efficient devices. Even though you may not feel it, the cost per feature in even a premium device like the iPhone has dropped substantially since its launch. The device size keeps shrinking all the time too. Cameras in phones have gotten substantially better and the battery lives longer too. How do they keep doing this? The secret is Moore's Law: the 1965 law states that processor speeds, or overall processing power for computers will double every two years meaning a reduction in the minimum transistor length used in the semiconductor "chips". These chips power the smart devices we use.

3 iOS

This is a mobile operating system created and developed by Apple Inc. exclusively for its hardware. It is the operating system that presently powers many of the company's mobile devices, including the iPhone, iPad, and iPod Touch.

4 Redbox VR

Information on this is available at: http://redboxvr.co.uk/

5 The Institute of Play

The Institute of Play set up a Quest to Learn school in New York in 2009. The school is organised around innovative technology-based instructional methods and the idea that digital games are central to the lives of today's children. It is part of a well-financed and carefully watched educational experiment by New York city on new models for schools.

Game designers take over structuring lessons so that they become a quest which blends skills from different areas of learning and experience. Students may have to balance budgets and brainstorm business ideas for an imaginary community or make architectural blueprints for a game they have to design. They are expected to learn skills like how to record podcasts, film and edit videos, play and design computer games and blog. In 2013, 56 percent of Quest middle-school students scored better than the citywide average on the state standardized English Language Arts exams, and 43 percent exceeded the citywide average for math. The Institute of Play offers online professional development programmes for teachers and downloadable resources for free. See, for example, https://docs.wixstatic.com/ugd/4401d6_745ff9d622a747ddab4994b dd86d7e2e.pdf

6 Google Arts and Culture

Information on this is available at: https://artsandculture.google.com/

7 OxSight

Information on this is available at: www.oxsight.co.uk/

8 Bose

Information on this is available at: https://developer.bose.com/content/tuning-augment ed-reality

9 What is a jig?

Information on this is available at: www.autismontario.com/Client/ASO/AO.nsf/object/ ASDVisualSupports/$file/ASDVisualSupports.pdf

10 Xiaoice

Information on this is available at: www.theverge.com/2018/5/22/17379508/microsoft-xiaoice-chat-bot-phone-call-demo

11 Partnership on AI

Information on this is available at: www.partnershiponai.org/

12 Bloom's Digital Taxonomy and the communication spectrum

In Human history we have seen many different ages, the dark ages, the middle ages and more recently the space and information ages. We live in a time that might best be described as the communication age.

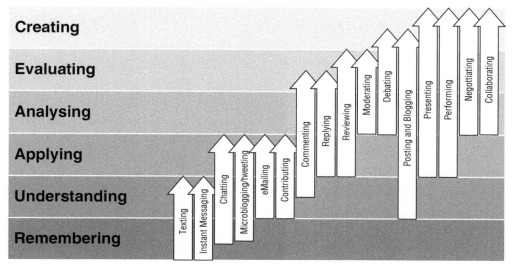

Collaboration is not a 21st Century skill, it is a 21st Century essential.

Figure 9.1 Bloom's Digital Taxonomy and the communication spectrum
Adapted from Andrew Churches

We are always connected, always available and constantly communicating and collaborating across a spectrum of activities with increasing levels of complexity and creativity.

13 Sunu band

Information on this is available at: www.sunu.io/en/index.html

14 MOOCs

These courses are available in the UK for free. Go to www.futurelearn.com/

Learners have 24/7 access to traditional course materials, such as readings and problem sets, plus interactive tools, such as videos, quizzes, user forums, social media chats and articles that all generate discussion and debate. Each course is open to anyone with internet access across the world.

15 MIT

With MIT you can earn a certificate in a multitude of topics and the online courses are free. For more information go to https://ocw.mit.edu/index.htm

16 The Khan Academy

This is a non-profit educational organization created in 2006 by educator Salman Khan with a goal of creating a set of free online tools that help educate students. It evolved from a single website for desktops to multiple apps available across many devices offer personalized learning across many subjects and every grade for anyone with internet access throughout the world. Its motto is: "You can learn anything. For free. For everyone. Forever."

The Khan Academy Lite (or KA Lite) is an open-source software that mimics the online experience of Khan Academy offline. If you don't have an internet connection you can watch Khan Academy videos, complete exercises, and check your progress by using KA lite. To inform others about these and to find out more go to www.khana cademy.org/or https://learningequality.org/ka-lite/

17 Soundbeam

Information on this is available at: www.soundbeam.co.uk/

18 Emotion Charades

Information on this is available at: www.indiegogo.com/projects/world-s-first-augment ed-reality-glasses-for-autism#/

19 Popar

Information on this is available at: https://popartoys.com/t/popar-smart-book

20 Clever Books

Information on this is available at: www.cleverbooks.eu/3d-flip-book/cleverbooks-prod ucts-catalog-education-2018/

21 Video of the robot, Pepper

www.youtube.com/watch?v=lqlyxg1-gE0

22 Report on use of neuro feedback

Y P C
Behaviour Support
3 July 2017
Report on Jon Doe
Effectiveness of Neuro Feedback Therapy

JD commenced neuro feedback therapy week commencing 15 April; he attends one session on a daily basis. Since attending his behaviour has improved immensely; he is calmer, listens to adults and takes on board reasons as to why things have to happen in such a way. He is happier in himself and appears to be less anxious.

SIMS Behaviour Records for JD since 25 April, a twelve-week period:

- 3 May disruptive behaviour (afternoon)
- 3 May fighting on yard (afternoon)
- 15 May verbal abuse to staff (afternoon)
- 6 June assault to staff (afternoon)

Of the above behaviours one incident needed to be logged in the bound and numbered book.*

SIMS behaviours logged in the previous 6 weeks (27 February–7 April) *before* commencing neuro feedback therapy.

- 3 March disruptive behaviour (am)
- 6 March assault on staff and students (am)
- 10 March assault on student (am)
- 13 March disruptive behaviour (pm)
- 16 March absconded (pm)
- 16 March assault on student (pm)
- 16 March verbal abuse on staff (pm)
- 21 March disruptive behaviour (pm)
- 21 March assault on student (am)
- 21 March disruptive behaviour (pm)
- 22 March disruptive behaviour (pm)

- 28 March assault on staff (am)
- 28 March disruptive behaviour (am)

Of the above incidents six incidents were logged in the bound and numbered book.*

BD-HLTA behaviour support

*A bound and numbered book is a record book that is designed to be the central reference point for recording the use of restraint. Restraint is about safeguarding students and staff. It is part of the team teach method of behaviour management. Information on this is available at: www.teamteach.co.uk/

23 Resources for download: school policies

Resource 1.1

iPad/Hand-Held Device – Acceptable Use Policy for a Special School

Date reviewed ....

The policies, procedures and information within this document applies to all iPads, iPods, VR phones, tablets or any other IT handheld device used in school. Teachers and other school staff may also set additional requirements for use within their classroom.

User's Responsibilities

Users must use protective covers/cases for their iPad.

The iPad screen is made of glass and therefore is subject to cracking and breaking if misused: Never drop nor place heavy objects (books, laptops, etc.) on top of the iPad.

Only a soft cloth or approved laptop screen cleaning solution is to be used to clean the iPad screen.

Do not subject the iPad to extreme heat or cold.

Do not store or leave unattended in vehicles.

Users may not photograph any other person, without that persons' consent.

The iPad is subject to routine monitoring by the school. Devices must be surrendered immediately upon request by any member of staff.

The school is not responsible for the financial or other loss of any personal files that may be deleted from an iPad.

Additional Responsibilities for Students

If an iPad is left at home or is not charged, the user remains responsible for completing all schoolwork as if they had use of their iPad.

Malfunctions or technical issues are not acceptable excuses for failing to return iPad to school daily.

Students must not use their iPad in School corridors on their journeys to and from school or outside of School buildings (unless with the teacher's permission).

Students in breach of the Responsible Use Policy may be subject to but not limited to;

disciplinary action, confiscation, removal of content or referral to external agencies in the event of illegal activity.

In the event of any disciplinary action, the completion of all class work remains the responsibility of the student.

Safeguarding and Maintaining as an Academic Tool

iPad batteries are required to be charged and be ready to use in school.

Syncing the iPad to iTunes or iCloud will be maintained by a school administrator.

Items deleted from the iPad cannot be recovered.

Memory space is limited. Academic content takes precedence over personal files and apps.

The whereabouts of the iPad should be known at all times.

It is a student's responsibility to keep their iPad safe and secure. If the student is unable to do this then the class staff take the responsibility.

iPads belonging to other students are not to be tampered within any manner.

If an iPad is found unattended, it should be given to the nearest member of staff.

Lost, Damaged or Stolen iPad

If the iPad is lost, stolen, or damaged, the ICT technicians/Network Manager/Head Teacher must be notified immediately.

iPads that are believed to be stolen can be tracked through iCloud.

Prohibited Uses (not exclusive):

Accessing Inappropriate Materials – All material on the iPad must adhere to the ICT Responsible Use Policy. Users are not allowed to send, access, upload, download or distribute offensive, threatening, pornographic, obscene, or sexually explicit materials.

Illegal Activities – Use of the school's internet/e-mail accounts for financial or commercial gain or for any illegal activity.

Violating Copyrights – Users are not allowed to violate copyrights.

Cameras – Users must use good judgment when using the camera. The user agrees that the camera will not be used to take inappropriate, illicit or sexually explicit photographs or videos, nor will it be used to embarrass anyone in any way. Any use of camera in toilets or changing rooms, regardless of intent, will be treated as a serious violation.

Images of other people may only be made with the permission of those in the photograph.

Posting of images/movie on the internet into a public forum is strictly forbidden, without the express permission of the teacher or in the case of staff use; a member of the Senior Leadership team.

Use of the camera and microphone is strictly prohibited unless permission is granted by a teacher.

Misuse

Misuse of Passwords, Codes or Other Unauthorized Access

Users/Class teachers are encouraged to set a passcode on iPads to prevent other users from misusing it.

Any user caught trying to gain access to another user's accounts, files or data will be subject to disciplinary action.

Malicious Use/Vandalism – Any attempt to destroy hardware, software or data will be subject to disciplinary action.

Jailbreaking – Jailbreaking is the process of which removes any limitations placed on the iPad by Apple. Jailbreaking results in a less secure device and is strictly prohibited.

Inappropriate media may not be used as a screensaver or background photo. Presence of pornographic materials, inappropriate language, alcohol, drug or gang related symbols or pictures will result in disciplinary actions.

Individual users are responsible for the setting up and use of any home internet connections and no support will be provided for this by the school.

Users should be aware of and abide by the guidelines set out by the School eSafety policy.

The school reserves the right to confiscate and search an iPad to ensure compliance with this iPad/Tablet Responsible Use Policy.

Resource 1.2 Parent agreement

If a pupil takes an iPad home a parent/carer must read and sign below:

I have read, understand and agree to abide by the terms of the iPad/Hand-Held Device Acceptable Use Policy.

Name ....   Signature ....

Date   ....

Pledge for iPad Use

I will take good care of the iPad.

I will never leave the iPad unattended.

I will never lend the iPad to others.

I will know where the iPad is at all times.

I will charge the iPad's battery every night.

I will keep food and drinks away from the iPad since they may cause damage to the device.

I will not disassemble any part of the iPad or attempt any repairs.

I will protect the iPad by only carrying it whilst it is in a case.

I will use the iPad in ways that are appropriate.

I understand that my iPad is subject to inspection at any time without notice. I will only photograph people with their permission.

I will only use the camera or the microphone when my teacher tells me to.

I will never share any images from the iPad.

If the iPad is broken whilst in the home the parent will pay for the repair.

Resource 1.3

Student E-Safety Policy for a special school

Date reviewed ....

INTRODUCTION

E-Safety encompasses internet technologies and electronic communications such as mobile phones as well as collaboration tools and personal publishing. It highlights the need to educate students about the benefits and risks of using technology and provides safeguards and awareness for users to enable them to control their online experience.

The school's E-Safety policy should operate in conjunction with other policies including those for Student behaviour, Bullying, Curriculum, Data Protection and Security.

E-Safety depends on effective practice at a number of levels:

–   Responsible ICT use by all staff and students; encouraged by education and made explicit through published policies.

–   Sound implementation of E-Safety policy in both administration and curriculum, including secure school network design and use.

–   Safe and secure internet access including the effective management of filtering systems.

Teaching and learning – Why internet use is important

–   The internet is an essential element in 21st century life for education, business and social interaction. The school has a duty to provide students with quality internet access as part of their learning experience.

–   Internet use is a part of the statutory curriculum and a necessary tool for staff and students.

Internet use will enhance learning

–   The school internet access will be designed expressly for student use and will include filtering appropriate to the age and needs of students.

–   If appropriate students will begin to learn about what internet use is acceptable and what is not, and given clear objectives for internet use.

–   Internet access will be planned to enrich and extend learning activities.

If appropriate students will be shown and taught how to evaluate internet content

- If staff or students discover unsuitable sites, the URL (address), time, date and content should be reported to the school ICT Coordinator.
- Staff should ensure that the use of internet derived materials by staff and by students complies with copyright law.

Managing internet access

- The security of the school information systems will be reviewed regularly.
- Virus protection will be installed and updated regularly.
- The school will have broadband with its firewall and filters.

Published content and the school web site

- The contact details on the website should be the school address, e-mail and telephone number. Staff or student's personal information will not be published.
- The head teacher will take overall editorial responsibility and ensure that content is accurate and appropriate.

Publishing student's images and work

- Photographs that include students will be selected carefully and all staff must be aware of the students at our school whose identity and pictures cannot be included in our website.
- Parents will have a private login section to view their own child's documents, photos and work. No one else, except the class teacher and school management will have access to these documents etc.
- Students' full names should not be used anywhere on the Web site, except for in private parental login sections
- Written permission from parents or carers will be obtained before photographs of students are published on the school Web site.
- Student's work should only be published with the permission of the student and parents.

Social networking and personal publishing

- Social networking sites and newsgroups will be blocked unless a specific use is approved.
- Students are advised never to give out personal details of any kind which may identify them or their location. Examples would include real name, address, mobile or

landline phone numbers, school, e-mail address, names of friends, specific interests and clubs etc.

— Students and parents will be advised that the use of social network spaces outside school may be inappropriate for primary aged students.

Managing filtering

— The school will work in partnership with the service provider to ensure filtering systems are as effective as possible.

— Senior management will ensure that checks are made to ensure that the filtering methods selected are appropriate, effective and reasonable.

Managing emerging technologies

— Emerging technologies will be examined for educational benefit and a risk assessment will be carried out before use in school is allowed.

— Mobile phones should not be brought to school by students unless teachers request them for a lesson in order to train students in acceptable use of phones, setting up phones, appropriate phone apps etc.

Protecting personal data

— Personal data will be recorded, processed, transferred and made available according to the Data Protection Act 1998.

— In common with other media such as magazines, books and video, some material available via the internet is unsuitable for students. The school will take all reasonable precautions to ensure that users access only appropriate material. However, due to the international scale and linked nature of internet content, it is not possible to guarantee that unsuitable material will never appear on a school computer.

— The head teacher will ensure that the E-Safety Policy is implemented and compliance with the policy monitored.

Handling E-Safety complaints

— Complaints of internet misuse will be dealt with by a senior member of staff.

— Any complaint about staff misuse must be referred to the head teacher.

— Complaints of a child protection nature must be dealt with in accordance with school child protection procedures.

— Students and parents will be informed of the Complaints Procedure.

Community use of the internet

- The school will be sensitive to internet related issues experienced by students out of school, e.g. social networking sites, and offer appropriate advice.
- Parents using school ICT equipment must sign an AUP consent form prior to use (e.g. Family ICT, Numeracy and Literacy).
- Children will take part in regular E-Safety session with PC Community Schools Liaison Officer.

Introducing the E-Safety policy to students

- Students will be informed that internet use will be monitored.
- Advice on E-Safety will be introduced at an ability -appropriate level to raise the awareness and importance of safe and responsible internet use.

Staff and the E-Safety policy

- All staff will be given the school Staff E-Safety Policy and Student E-Safety Policy and have their importance explained.
- Staff should be aware that internet traffic can be monitored and traced to the individual user.

Discretion and professional conduct is essential.

Staff will be guided towards the Hwb online safety platform https://hwb.gov.wales/onlinesafety

Enlisting parents'/carers' support

- Parents'/carers' attention will be drawn to the School E-Safety Policy in a newsletter.
- Parents will be given advice as to which online sites can support them with their child's use of the internet: https://hwb.gov.wales/onlinesafety/parents-and-carers.
- Parents will be offered E-Safety training in school with the PC community liaison officer.

Resource 1.4

Electronic Communications Acceptable Use Policy for a special school

Date policy reviewed ....

This policy will be reviewed annually. It will be agreed by the school's management team and approved by governors.

IMPORTANCE OF THE USE OF ELECTRONIC COMMUNICATION

*   The purpose of using electronic communication in schools is to raise educational standards, to support the professional development and work of staff, and to enhance the school's business administration.

*   Access to electronic communication systems is a necessary tool for staff and an entitlement for students.

*   It should be noted that the use of a computer system without permission or for a purpose not agreed by the school could constitute a criminal offence under the Computer Misuse Act 1990.

The use of a computer system without permission or for a purpose not agreed by the school may constitute a criminal offence under the Data Protection Act 1998 or Computer Misuse Act 1990.

BENEFITS TO THE SCHOOL

Access to world-wide educational resources including museums and art galleries;

Inclusion in government initiatives. such as Virtual Teacher Centre and community grids for learning;

Information, collaboration and cultural exchanges between students world-wide;

News and current events;

Cultural, social and leisure use in libraries, clubs and at home;

Discussion with experts in many fields for students and staff;

Staff professional development – access to educational materials and good curriculum practice plus a means for staff to access training materials and receive mentor support;

Communication with colleagues, the advisory and support services, professional associations and support groups; Exchange of curriculum and administration data with local authorities and Government.

ASSESSING RISKS

In common with other media such as magazines, books and video, some material available via electronic communication and the internet in particular is unsuitable for students.

It is not possible to provide a 100% check of the contents of electronic messages for every word or phrase or picture that might be considered unsuitable.

The school will supervise students and take all reasonable precautions to ensure that users access only appropriate material.

However, due to the international scale and linked nature of information available via the internet, it is not possible to guarantee that particular types of material will never appear on a screen. Neither the school nor the County Council can accept liability for the material accessed, or any consequences thereof.

*   Methods to quantify and minimise the risk will be reviewed.

*   Staff, parents and governors will work with education officers to establish and maintain procedures so that every reasonable measure is being taken to ensure acceptable use.

*   The Head teacher will ensure that the policy is implemented effectively. The senior management team will regularly monitor implementation of the policy.

*   Exceptional examples of good practice will be communicated to the local authority's ICT Adviser so they may be disseminated to other schools.

Should examples of unacceptable use arise these will be communicated immediately, electronically or in writing, to the ICT Adviser so that appropriate steps can be taken to prevent future occurrences of such use.

AUTHORISING INTERNET ACCESS

*   Internet access is a necessary part of planned lessons. It is an entitlement for students based on responsible use.

*   Dependent upon the needs of the student access to the internet may be by teacher or adult demonstration.

*   Students will access teacher-approved/prepared materials.

*   Students may access teacher-approved/prepared materials before being given supervised access to the internet.

*   Dependent upon the student needs internet access may be granted to a whole class as part of the scheme of work after a suitable introduction to the rules for responsible use of the internet.

* Teachers will monitor and control access by students via a shared identity and password.

* Anyone undertaking personal study will be required to apply for internet access individually, by signing an Electronic Communication Acceptable Use Statement

* A record will be maintained of all staff and students with internet access. Staff and students will be removed from the record when access is no longer required and has been stopped.

* The school will, where appropriate, record permission for access on a whole-class basis.

* Parents will be informed that students will be provided with supervised access to electronic communication where it is important to their education.

* Parents will be asked to sign and return a permission form for use of electronic communication.

SECURITY

Security strategies will be discussed with the local authority and will take account of the local authority policies, guidelines from the ICT department and the relevant legal framework.

* The IT System Manager will ensure that the agreed security measures are implemented.

* The security of the whole system will be regularly reviewed with regard to threats to security resulting from use of electronic communication.

* Personal data transmitted electronically will be encrypted or otherwise secured.

* Virus protection will be installed, updated regularly and used in accordance with agreed security procedures.

* Use of memory sticks will not be used in school and staff will save data to their own file on the school website so that they are able to safely access information from home.

* Use of electronic communication to send attachments, such as software updates, print drivers and system utilities, will be monitored and regularly reviewed.

EFFECTIVE LEARNING AND THE USE OF ELECTRONIC COMMUNICATION

The school will work with the local authority and relevant officers of the County Council to ensure systems to protect students are reviewed and improved.

* Internet access will be planned to enrich and extend learning activities as an integrated aspect of the curriculum.

* Students will be given appropriate and clear objectives for internet use.

* Students will be informed of relevant and suitable Web sites.

* Students will be guided and educated in taking responsibility for internet access.

* Students will be informed that checks can be made on files held on the system and on access to remote computers.

* Students using the internet will be supervised appropriately.

* Internet access will be via the local authority's networks, which provides a service designed for student and staff use. This will include filtering appropriate to the age of students and timed access to match agreed needs.

ASSESSING CONTENT ON THE INTERNET

* Students will be made aware that the writer of an electronic mail message or the author of a Web page may not be the person claimed or the intended recipient.

* Students will be taught to use search engines appropriately.

* Students will be encouraged to tell a teacher immediately if they encounter any material that makes them feel uncomfortable.

* When copying materials from the Web students will be shown how to comply with copyright.

* Students will be taught to check information before accepting it as true, an important aspect of higher level teaching.

MANAGING E-MAIL USE

* Students are expected to use e-mail if possible as part of the curriculum.

* Communications with persons and organisations will be managed to ensure appropriate educational use and that the good name of the school is maintained.

* The forwarding of chain letters will be banned and students will be shown why they are dangerous.

* Students may send e-mail as part of planned lessons.

* In-coming e-mail for groups of students will be regarded as public.

* E-mail messages on school business (e.g. arranging a work placement) must be approved before sending.

* E-mail messages on school business will only be transmitted from a school e-mail address – not an individual e-mail address.

* External e-mail users should be encouraged to send initial messages to a school

E-mail address rather than an individual e-mail address. Subsequent contact, once approved, is likely to be via an individual who has her/his own e-mail address or a class/group with its own address.

* Students may only attach files to e-mail messages with the approval of a teacher and only then if the files are free from viruses.

MANAGING EMERGING TECHNOLOGIES

Many emerging communications technologies offer the potential to develop new teaching and learning tools, including mobile communications, wide internet access and multimedia. A risk assessment needs to be undertaken on each new technology and effective practice in classroom use developed. The safest approach is to deny access until a risk assessment has been completed and safety demonstrated.

* Emerging technologies will be examined for educational benefit and a risk assessment will be carried out before use in school is allowed.

* A risk assessment will be undertaken on each new technology and effective practice in classroom use developed.

* Use of cellular wireless, infrared and Bluetooth communication is only allowed within the context of the agreed policy.

MANAGING VIDEO CONFERENCING

Video conferencing enables users to see and hear each other between different locations. It is a 'real time' interactive technology and has many uses in education.

The National Educational Network (NEN) has been developed. This is a secure, broadband, IP network interconnecting the ten regional school's networks across England with the Welsh, Scottish and the Northern Irish networks. Schools can thus use IP technology in a secure and managed environment. Video conferences, within and outside the county should be undertaken via the videoconferencing booking system. In exceptional circumstances a video conference with another local school may be undertaken using a direct IP connection.

The equipment and network

* All videoconferencing equipment in the classroom must be switched off when not in use and not set to auto answer.

* The internet will not be used for video conferencing because it is not managed by a single responsible agency and there is no inherent security. External IP addresses will not be made available to other sites.

* Video conferencing contact information will not be put on the school web site.

Users

*   Video conferencing will be supervised appropriately for the students' age and ability. Parents and guardians must agree for their children to take part in video conferences – via the standard consent form.

*   Unique log on and password details for educational video conferencing services will only be issued to members of staff and kept secure.

*   Establish dialogue with other conference participants before taking part in a video conference. If it is a non-school site it is important to check that they are delivering material that is appropriate to the students.

*   When recording a lesson, written permission will have been given by all sites and participants. The reason for the recording will be given and the recording of video conference will be made clear to all parties at the start of the conference.

Recorded material will be stored securely.

*   If third-party materials are to be included, checks will be made to ensure that recording is acceptable to avoid infringing the owners' Intellectual Property Rights (IPR).

MANAGING FILE TRANSFERS

File transfer is the process of moving files across the internet and is referred to as FTP (File Transfer Protocol). Downloading is the process of copying a file from the internet to your computer. Uploading is the process of copying a file from your computer to a computer (usually a server) on the internet. Care must be taken to ensure that files uploaded are suitable for their intended purpose and free from viruses. Similarly, any files downloaded must be appropriate for identified needs, validly obtained and checked for viruses before use.

*   File transfer will be undertaken subject to restrictions imposed via the local Firewall and may be limited to designated PCs/individuals.

*   Schools will not transfer files directly to another school but will deposit the file on a server at the local authorities' ICT department from where the receiving school will collect the file.

*   File transfer will only be carried out by staff.

*   File transfer will only be made by students under the direct supervision of a member of staff.

*   All files downloaded will appropriate to educational use or technical needs and both licensing and copyright requirements will be met.

*   All files downloaded will only be used if they are found to be free from viruses.

* All files uploaded will be suitable for their intended purpose and free from viruses.

PUBLISHING ON THE WEB

* The Head teacher will delegate editorial responsibility to a designated group of staff to ensure that content is accurate and quality of presentation is maintained.
* The Web site will comply with the school's guidelines for publications.
* All material must be the author's own work.
* Work included that is not the author's should be credited with a statement giving the author's identity or status.
* The point of contact on the Web site will be the school address and telephone number.
* Home information or individual e-mail addresses will not be published.
* No personal information or individual e-mail addresses will be published.
* Photographs of identifiable individual students will not be published on the Web site.
* Group photographs will not have a name list attached.

APPROPRIATE AND SAFE INTERNET ACCESS

* Screens used by students will be in public view to staff and students in the same group.
* Staff will check that the sites selected for student use are appropriate to the age and maturity of students.
* Senior staff will monitor and regularly review the effectiveness of access strategies for electronic communication.
* Staff will ensure that occasional checks are made on files to monitor compliance with the school's Electronic Communications Acceptable Use Policy.
* A range of fully tested approved sites will be copied to the school intranet.

HANDLING COMPLAINTS

* Responsibility for handling incidents will be given to a member of the senior management team or the Head teacher as appropriate.
* If staff or students discover unsuitable sites, the URL (address) and content will be reported to the ICT department in the local authority. They will immediately prevent access to any site considered unsuitable. An urgent investigation will be undertaken by them, in consultation with audit and legal staff, as defined within agreed

procedures. Appropriate action will be taken and there may be occasions when the police must be contacted. Parents and students will need to work in partnership with staff to resolve any issue.

* Sanctions available include interview by a senior member of staff and, if appropriate, informing parents or carers.

* A student may have electronic communication access or computer access denied for a period.

* Denial of access could include all school work held on the system, including any examination work.

* Students and parents will be informed of the Complaints Procedure.

KEEPING STAFF, STUDENTS AND PARENTS INFORMED

* Rules for internet access will be available on the school file server. The Acceptable Use Statement and Rules for Responsible Use will be available in the same location.

* All staff including teachers, supply staff, classroom assistants and support staff, will be provided with the Electronic Communication Acceptable Use Policy and its importance explained.

* Parents' attention will be drawn to the Policy in newsletters, the school brochure and on the school intranet and Web sites.

* Responsible use of electronic communication, covering both school and home use, will be covered with all students at the beginning of each school year.

ENLISTING PARENT SUPPORT

* Guidelines for parents on issues such as safe use of internet and electronic mail will be established. along with details of the school's Electronic Communication Acceptable Use Policy.

* Training will regularly be provided for parents.

* A careful balance will be maintained between keeping parents informed and raising issues of concern.

REMOTE ACCESS

Remote access from the local authority's ICT department to computers in school will allow problems and performance to be investigated without the need for a visit to school. Additionally, new and updated software can be downloaded directly and quickly to computers in school. File servers in school will be able to automatically log, with the ICT department, potential faults before they occur. This will allow preventative action to be taken to ensure continuity of operation. The ability to give technical support in this way will result in provision of faster, more efficient, higher quality and best value services.

The confidentiality of school data must clearly be retained and access should only be undertaken by approved staff following authorisation from the school. In using remote access, the principle adopted should be that the action being taken is exactly the same as would be carried out of the support was given by visiting the school.

* Remote access (where available) to school computers and managed network hubs will be given only to appropriate staff from the ICT department and will be subject to prior arrangement and provision of a record of work carried out.

* All remote access will be subject to the local authority Commitment Statement.

WIDER ACCESS IN THE COMMUNITY

The internet is available in many situations in the local community. In addition to the home, access may be available at the local library, youth club, adult education centre, village hall, supermarket or cyber café. Ideally, young people would encounter a consistent policy to internet use wherever they are.

In local libraries and youth and community centres, internet access by students of school age is managed by the local authority's ICT department with the same filtering and monitoring software that is employed for internet access from schools.

In community internet access there is a fine balance to be achieved in ensuring 'freedom of information' whilst providing adequate protection for children and others who may be offended by inappropriate material.

The school will be sensitive to internet related issues experienced by students out of school, e.g. social networking sites, and offer appropriate advice.

Resource 1.5

POLICY ON THE USE OF PHONES INCLUDING MOBILE PHONES IN THE SCHOOL BUILDING

Special School (for students aged 4 to 11 years of age)

Private Mobile Phones – Use by Staff

Date Reviewed ....

STAFF

If Staff need to make an outgoing telephone call which is school business, then the Office phones should be used.

If Staff are expecting incoming telephone calls relating to school business the school number (******) should be given so that if you are not available, then a message can be taken by office staff. Staff should not give out their mobile number for such use during the day.

Staff should ensure that their mobile phones are switched off in school during the school day i.e. 9:30am – 4:00pm. If staff want to make outgoing calls using their mobile phones they may do so but only during lunch time when not on duty and out of school hours.

USE BY STUDENTS

There is usually no reason why a student should need to use a mobile phone in school during the school day. There is therefore no reason for a student to bring a mobile phone to school. Use of phones outside of class can only be granted with permission by the head teacher and under very strict conditions.

If phones are to be used as part of a lesson then parental agreement will be sought for example if students are being given guidance on setting up a phone or how to use a phone for educational or safety reasons, then the phone may be brought into school for instruction purposes with parents' consent.

Students bringing their own mobile phones to school should be asked to take it to the Heads Office.

If a student needs to contact home for whatever reason, then this should be done under strict supervision by a member of staff and the reason for the call must be verified.

School Telephones – Private use by Staff

All staff should ensure that incoming private calls to ****** are restricted to emergency calls only.

If staff need to make an outgoing private call (during free time) this may be done at the office. Staff are expected to make a payment for the use of the phone. Office staff need to be consulted regarding this.

Use of Fax for Private Communications

The fax should not be used for private communications without permission of the head teacher.

Use of Fax and Phones for School Business.

It is legitimate to use any of the above-mentioned equipment on school business.

References

Anderson, A. (2016) Available online at https://onlinelibrary.wiley.com/doi/pdf/10.1111/1471-3802.12174

ASSOA (2018) Available online at www.assoa.nt.edu.au/the-school/our-school/

Australian Online Safety Education. Available online at www.esafety.gov.au

BBC (2018) Available online at www.bbc.co.uk/sport/olympics/43893891

Blue Room Research Team. "Investigating the effectiveness of virtual reality treatment for specific phobia and fear in children with ASD", The Blue Room Project, Newcastle University. Available online at http://bit.ly/sc235-32

Brown, D. (2012) "Sensory Confusion", reSources, California Deaf Blind Services. Available online at http://files.cadbs.org/200002015-16edb17e69/SensoryConfusion.pdf

CNBC (2017) Available online at www.cnbc.com/2017/03/28/microsoft-google-and-facebook-see-billions-in-future-of-education.html

Corbett, S. (2010) "Learning by Playing: Video Games in the Classroom", *The New York Times*. Available online at www.nytimes.com/2010/09/19/magazine/19video-t.html

Didehbani, N. (2016) Available online at www.utdallas.edu/news/2016/9/22-32196_Virtual-Reality-Helps-Children-on-Autism-Spectrum-story-wide.html

Donaldson, G. (2015) "Successful Futures. Independent Review of Curriculum and Assessment Arrangements in Wales". Welsh Government.

Dube, R. (2014) "Plugging in Your Brain and Body–The Future of Implanted Computers". Available online at www.makeuseof.com/tag/plugging-brain-body-future-implanted-computers/

Dunn, W. (2017) "Autistic hackers: the teenagers who 'get carried away'", *The New Statesman*. Available online at ww.newstatesman.com/microsites/cyber/2017/10/will-prison-deter-autistic-teenager-hacking

Durie, B. (2005) "Senses special: Doors of perception", *The New Statesman*. Available online at www.newscientist.com/article/mg18524841-600-senses-special-doors-of-perception/

Finley, K. (2014) "Wanna Build Your Own Google? Visit the App Store for Algorithms", *Wired*, 11 August 2014. Available online at www.wired.com/2014/08/algorithmia/

Gambino, M. (2009) "A Salute to the Wheel", *Smithsonian.com*. Available online at www.smithsonianmag.com/science-nature/a-salute-to-the-wheel-31805121/

Gardner, H. (1993) *Frames of Mind: The Theory of Multiple Intelligences*. London; Fontana Press.

Gates, B. and Gates, M. (2006) "The Silent Epidemic: Perspectives of High School Dropouts". Available online at www.gatesfoundation.org/Media-Center/Press-Releases/2006/03/Americas-Silent-Dropout-Epidemic

Georgopoulos, V. C., Malandraki, G. A. and Stylios, C. D. (2003) "A fuzzy cognitive map approach to differential diagnosis of specific language impairment", *Journal of Artificial Intelligence in Medicine*, pp. 261–278.

Grandin, T. and Scariano, M. M. (1996) *Emergence: Labeled Autistic*. USA: Grand Central Publishing.

Grayling, C. (2013) Available online at www.gov.uk/government/speeches/crime-in-context-speech

Green, H. and Hannon, C. (2007) *Space. Education for a Digital Generation*. London: Demos.

Heath, A. (2017) Available online at http://uk.businessinsider.com/facebook-smart-glasses-ar-oculus-patent-2017-8

Holley, P. (2017) "Stephen Hawking just moved up humanity's deadline for escaping Earth", *Independent.co.uk*. Available online at www.independent.co.uk/news/science/stephen-hawking-just-moved-up-humanitys-deadline-for-escaping-earth-a7722181.html

Josman, N. and Weiss, T. (2008) "Haifa Research Team: Effectiveness of Virtual Reality for Teaching Street-Crossing Skills to Children and Adolescents with Autism", Haifa University. Available online at http://bit.ly/sc235-33

King, M.L. (1963) Available online at www.let.rug.nl/usa/documents/1951-/martin-luther-kings-i-have-a-dream-speech-august-28-1963.php

Koizumi, A. et al. (2016) "Fear reduction without fear through reinforcement of neural activity that bypasses conscious exposure", *Nature Human Behaviour*. DOI:10.1038/S41562-016-0006. Available online at www.cam.ac.uk/research/news/reconditioning-the-brain-to-overcome-fear

Lanier, J. (2017) *Dawn of the New Everything: A Journey through Virtual Reality*, eBook; Vintage Penguin.

NAS (2018) Available online at www.autism.org.uk/about/in-education/exclusion/permanent-england.aspx

Ndopo, Edward K http://www.africanleadershipacademy.org/gsie-a-call-to-action/

Ofcom (2017) Available online at www.ofcom.org.uk/__data/assets/pdf_file/0020/108182/children-parents-media-use-attitudes-2017.pdf

Orndorff-Plunkett, F., Singh, F., Aragón, O.R. and Pineda, J. A. (2017) "Assessing the Effectiveness of Neurofeedback Training in the Context of Clinical and Social Neuroscience", *Brain Sciences Journal*. Available online at www.ncbi.nlm.nih.gov/pmc/articles/PMC5575615/

Papert, S. (1980) *Mindstorms: Children, Computers, and Powerful Ideas*. New York: Basic Books.

Piaget, J. (1974) *To Understand is to Invent: The Future of Education*. London: Penguin.

Prensky, M. (2016) "Unleashing the Power of Our 21st Century Kids through an *Education To Better Their World*". SNS Newsletter.

Richie, N. (2017) "World Changers". Available online at childmags.com.au

Robinson, P. (2016) "Remembering 'Pokémon Go', the Craze that Swept July 2016", Vice LLC. Available online at www.vice.com/en_uk/article/xdmpgq/remembering-pokemon-go-the-craze-that-swept-july-2016

Sanders, J. (2015) Available online at http://blog.whooosreading.org/10-classroom-rules-for-using-technology/

Schwab, K. (2017) *The Fourth Industrial Revolution*. Geneva, Switzerland: Portfolio Penguin.

Scott, K. (2018) "Did You Know–Shift Happens 2018 remix". Available online at www.youtube.com/watch?v=TwtS6Jy3ll8

SWfGL Available online at https://swgfl.org.uk

Voyager, D. (2018) Available online at https://danielvoyager.wordpress.com/sl-stats/

Wong, R. (2018) Available online at https://mashable.com/2018/05/08/microsoft-hololens-field-of-view-big-weakness/?europe=true#42SMYDzAGgqD

Index